noodles *to* pasta

noodles *to* pasta

fresh and easy recipes
with noodles, pasta and rice

Lynne Mullins
photography by **Louise Lister**

HarperCollinsPublishers

For Dad

HarperCollins*Publishers*

First published in Australia in 1999
by HarperCollins*Publishers* Pty Limited
ACN 009 913 517
A member of the HarperCollins*Publishers* (Australia) Pty Limited Group
http.//www.harpercollins.com.au

HarperCollinsPublishers
25 Ryde Road, Pymble, Sydney NSW 2073, Australia
31 View Road, Glenfield, Auckland 10, New Zealand
77–85 Fulham Palace Road, London W6 8JB, United Kingdom
Hazelton Lanes, 55 Avenue Road, Suite 2900, Toronto, Ontario M5R 3L2
and 1995 Markham Road, Scarborough, Ontario M1B 5M8, Canada
10 East 53rd Street, New York NY 10032, USA

National Library Cataloguing-in-Publication data:

Mullins, Lynne.
   Noodles to pasta: fresh and easy recipes with noodles, pasta and rice
   Includes index
   ISBN 0 7322 6752 8.
1. Cookery (Pasta). 2. Cookery (Rice). 3. Cookery –
Australia. 4. Noodles. I. Lister, Louise. II. Title.

Cover and internal photography by Louise Lister
Styling by Karen Cotton
Typeset in Stone Sans 11/16
Printed in Hong Kong by South China Printing Co. on 128gsm Matt Art

5 4 3 2 1
01 00 99

contents

foreword

I first knew Lynne Mullins as a talented private cook whom we featured in the pages of *Vogue Entertaining*. She stood out then for the focused enthusiasm that was to take her into a successful professional career, travelling widely and learning from the international masters. Later, as editor of *Australian Gourmet Traveller*, I have been delighted to have Lynne as a regular contributor whose delicate touch with food has put many of her creations on our covers.

Lynne combines an understanding of classical cooking with a keen sense of the needs of today's busy cooks. This timely book encompasses the way we want to eat now.

Carolyn Lockhart
Editor
Australian Gourmet Traveller

with
parmesan

mushroom risotto

Every European summer the Gritti Palace in Venice conducts cooking courses for visitors and guests. Chef Celestino Giacomella demonstrated a superb risotto when porcini mushrooms had just come into season and were piled high in ancient wooden boxes at the Rialto markets.

A mixture of fresh field and cultivated mushrooms works just as well.

5 tablespoons butter
1 medium onion, finely chopped
400 g (2 cups) Arborio rice
200 ml (¾ cup) dry white wine
1.5–1.75 litres (3–4 pints) hot chicken stock
400 g (14 oz) mixed mushrooms, sliced
80 g (½ cup) parmesan, grated
extra shaved parmesan

Melt 3 tablespoons butter in a large saucepan and add onion. Stir over medium heat until onion is pale yellow. Add rice and stir until coated with butter, add wine and stir.

Cook, stirring constantly until wine has evaporated. Stir in 2 ladles of chicken stock or enough to cover the rice. Stir over medium heat until stock has been absorbed. Continue cooking and stirring rice, adding stock a ladle at a time until absorbed. When rice is half cooked, add mushrooms. Continue cooking, stirring and adding stock until rice is cooked but firm to the bite, about 15 minutes. Stir in parmesan and remaining butter. Serve immediately with extra parmesan.

Serves 4

tomato sauce
for pasta

This is a quick-and-easy variation of a Marcella Hazan recipe that goes well with commercial pasta. Its concentrated flavour comes from the use of fresh tomatoes; however when they are not in season, substitute a 400 g (14 oz) can of plum (Roma) tomatoes and simmer for about 45 minutes instead of 20 minutes. The sauce quantities are sufficient for six diners.

4 tablespoons olive oil
1 medium onion, finely chopped
1 carrot, finely chopped
2 sticks celery, finely chopped
leaves from 2 sprigs flat-leaf (Italian) parsley
1 kg (2 lb) ripe plum (Roma) tomatoes, chopped
salt and pepper to taste
½ teaspoon caster (superfine) sugar

Place olive oil and onion in a large saucepan and cook over low heat until translucent. Add carrot, celery and parsley and cook, stirring occasionally until vegetables are soft.

Add tomatoes, salt, pepper and sugar and cook over low heat for about 20 minutes or until vegetables are cooked. Remove mixture and cool. Blend in a food processor.

Makes 2 cups

farfalle with chervil, artichokes and prosciutto

Baked ricotta can be purchased from quality delicatessens, however, it is very easy to make.
  Preheat the oven to 200°C. Place fresh ricotta in a lightly oiled ovenproof dish. Sprinkle with a little extra-virgin olive oil and pepper and bake for about 20 minutes or until firm and browned around the edges.

600 g (1¼ lb) farfalle (bow-shaped) pasta
60 ml (¼ cup) olive oil
150 g (5 oz) prosciutto, cut into strips
1 clove garlic, finely chopped
1 tomato, peeled and chopped
200 g (7 oz) artichokes in oil, drained and quartered
salt and black pepper
2 tablespoons fresh chervil, chopped
50 g (1½ oz) baked ricotta, coarsely grated
extra chervil leaves for garnish

Cook pasta in a large saucepan of salted boiling water until *al dente*. Drain.

Meanwhile, heat oil in a large frying pan and cook prosciutto and garlic over medium heat for 2 minutes. Add tomato and stir to combine. Add artichokes and season to taste with salt and black pepper. Add chervil and half the ricotta and then pasta. Cook until heated through, stirring gently to combine. Serve immediately, topped with remaining ricotta and extra chervil.

Serves 4

with parmesan

risi e bisi

Spending a week in a grand palazzo in Venice having lessons with renowned Italian cooking teacher, Fulvia Sesani, I hardly noticed that it rained heavily the entire week.

'Risi e Bisi is not a soup, not a risotto but a wave,' said Fulvia, explaining the consistency of this dish, which is best cooked with fresh peas.

4 tablespoons butter
75 g (2½ oz) pancetta, chopped
1 small onion, chopped
400 g (2 cups) Arborio rice
2 cups shelled fresh green peas
1.75–2 litres (1¾–2 quarts) hot chicken stock
2 tablespoons chopped flat-leaf (Italian) parsley
1 teaspoon fennel seeds
80 g (½ cup) parmesan, grated
extra grated parmesan

Place 2 tablespoons of butter in a large saucepan and melt over medium heat. Add pancetta and onion and stir until onion is soft. Add the rice and cook, stirring for 2–3 minutes. Add the peas and a couple of ladles of chicken stock and stir. Continue adding stock, a few ladles at a time, and stirring over medium heat for about 15 minutes or until the rice is tender but firm to the bite.

Remove from heat and stir in parsley, fennel seeds, parmesan and remaining butter. Serve hot with additional parmesan.

Serves 4

penne puttanesca

This colourful spicy dish doesn't need parmesan to finish, just a generous sprinkling of parsley or basil or both, and perhaps a little extra chilli if desired. Use the superior anchovies in salt if available – rinse well before using.

500 g (1 lb) penne pasta
2 tablespoons olive oil
2 cloves garlic, finely chopped
4 large ripe tomatoes, peeled and chopped
12 kalamata olives, pitted and sliced
a pinch of caster (superfine) sugar
2 tablespoons flat-leaf (Italian) parsley, chopped
3 anchovy fillets, chopped
2 tablespoons capers, roughly chopped
1 teaspoon dried chilli flakes or to taste
salt to taste

Cook penne in plenty of salted boiling water until *al dente*. Drain.

Heat olive oil in a large pan over medium heat and add garlic. Stir until aromatic. Add tomatoes, olives, sugar, 1 tablespoon of parsley, anchovies, capers, chilli flakes and salt and cook for about 10 minutes, stirring frequently.

Pour tomato sauce over pasta, toss well to combine and serve topped with remaining parsley.

Serves 4

with parmesan

spaghetti with curly endive, italian sausage and olives

500 g (1 lb) spaghetti
4 Italian sausages (about 80 g/2½ oz each)
3 tablespoons olive oil
1 leek, finely sliced
2 cloves garlic, finely chopped
1 bunch curly endive, torn into pieces
dried chilli flakes to taste
12 kalamata olives, pitted and sliced
2 tablespoons parmesan, grated

Cook pasta in a large saucepan of salted boiling water until *al dente*. Drain.

Cook sausages in a non-stick frying pan over medium heat. Drain and slice. Heat olive oil in a large pan and cook leek and garlic until leek is half cooked.

Add curly endive and cook until wilted. Add the pasta and chilli flakes and stir to combine. Serve topped with olives and parmesan.

Serves 4

leek risotto

Leeks are great as a cooked vegetable and also for flavouring soups. Use small leeks where possible as they have a superior flavour and texture. Italian Arborio rice is a pearly white, short-grained variety that is ideal for risotto as it absorbs liquid readily while the grains remain firm and chewy.

1 leek, chopped
100 g (½ cup) butter
150 g (¾ cup) Arborio rice
2 tablespoons white wine
500–750 ml (2–3 cups) chicken stock, simmering
½ tomato, chopped
1 tablespoon finely chopped flat-leaf (Italian) parsley
2 tablespoons parmesan, grated
2 plum (Roma) tomatoes

Cook leek in half the butter over low heat until soft. Add rice and stir until it is well coated. Add wine and stir until absorbed. Gradually stir in the chicken stock, one ladle at a time, allowing each addition to be absorbed before adding the next. Cook until the rice is tender but firm to the bite and creamy.

Fold in the tomato and parsley. Remove from the heat and stir in the remaining butter and parmesan. Cut the tomatoes into 3 wedges and place under a hot grill or fry in a little hot olive oil until cooked. Garnish with tomato wedges.

Serves 2

fettuccine alfredo

This simple dish is a favourite in my family. During the truffle season in Piedmont I enjoyed it at La Camilla where Valentina Harris was teaching for the Tasting Italy Cooking School. She added shavings of fresh white truffle as a topping, which was superb. My variation is tasty without the truffles but requires the best Parmigiano-Reggiano or at least *grana* cheese.

500 g (1 lb) fettuccine
100 g (½ cup) butter, chopped
375 ml (1½ cups) pouring cream
160 g (1 cup) Parmigiano-Reggiano, freshly grated
salt and cracked black pepper
2 tablespoons finely chopped flat-leaf (Italian) parsley
extra shaved Parmigiano-Reggiano

Cook pasta in a large saucepan of salted boiling water until *al dente*. Drain.

Combine butter, cream and Parmigiano-Reggiano in a medium-sized saucepan and stir over low heat until boiling. Add salt, pepper and parsley and stir. Pour over pasta and toss well to combine. Serve topped with extra shaved parmesan.

Serves 4

bucatini with
four cheeses

Bucatini is a hollow pasta similar to spaghetti. The inspiration for this recipe came from the luxurious Villa D'Este Hotel on Lake Como in Italy's north. Luciano Parolari and Jean Govoni Salvadore are both excellent cooks and have taught me many secrets of northern Italian cuisine. This sauce can be made in minutes.

500 g (1 lb) bucatini
2 teaspoons butter
3 rashers bacon, chopped
1 clove garlic, finely chopped
100 g (½ cup) edam, diced
100 g (½ cup) gruyère, diced
100 g (½ cup) fontina, diced
250 ml (1 cup) pouring cream
4 tablespoons tomato passata (see glossary)
1 tablespoon chopped flat-leaf (Italian) parsley
cracked black pepper
80 g (½ cup) parmesan, grated

Cook pasta in a large saucepan of salted boiling water until *al dente*. Drain.

Melt butter in a pan and add bacon and garlic and stir over medium heat. When bacon is cooked add edam, gruyère and fontina with the cream and stir until the cheeses melt.

Add tomato passata, parsley and pepper. Cook over low heat for 2–3 minutes. Pour the sauce over drained pasta, add parmesan and toss to combine. Serve immediately.

Serves 4

carla's parmesan tart

Carla Tomasi is a very friendly, generous chef of Roman heritage who specialises in Sicilian cuisine. Tasting Places Cooking School organises cooking holidays at Villa Ravida in Menfi, Sicily, with Carla in charge of the stoves and the students. This is one of her delicious dishes. I prefer to make the pastry in the food processor but it works equally well when made by hand.

Pastry

225 g (1½ cups) plain (all-purpose) flour
100 g (½ cup) unsalted butter, cubed
1 teaspoon salt
2–3 tablespoons iced water

Filling

1 tablespoon extra-virgin olive oil
1 bunch spring onions (scallions), trimmed and cut into 5 cm (2 in) lengths
salt and pepper
250 ml (1 cup) pouring cream
4 large eggs
200 g (1¼ cups) Parmigiano-Reggiano, grated
4 tablespoons sour cream
4 tablespoons milk
8 sun-dried tomatoes, finely sliced

To make the pastry, place flour, butter and salt in a food processor and blend until the mixture resembles coarse breadcrumbs. Add water and process until the mixture forms a ball. Remove, knead lightly and roll out on a lightly floured surface.

Line a 23 cm (9 in) flan tin with the pastry and rest, covered, in the refrigerator for 30 minutes. Preheat the oven to 200°C (400°F).

Line the shell with baking paper and then fill with dried beans, rice or pastry weights and bake for 10–12 minutes or until the pastry is golden and dry. Cool.

To make the filling, heat olive oil in a pan over medium heat and sauté spring onions until wilted. Season with salt and pepper. Set aside to cool.

Add cream to a large bowl and mix in eggs, one at a time, beating well after each addition. Add Parmigiano-Reggiano, sour cream, milk and sun-dried tomatoes. Add salt and pepper to taste. Pour cream mixture into pastry shell and arrange spring onions on top. Bake for 30–40 minutes or until cooked and golden.

Serves 8

macaroni with
asparagus and ham

Many Italians consider Bologna the gastronomic capital of Italy, where the origins of many dishes come from peasant cooking.

500 g (1 lb) macaroni
2 tablespoons butter
1 onion, sliced
1 bunch asparagus (about 200 g/7 oz), cut into
  1 cm (½ in) lengths and blanched
300 g (10 oz) ham, diced
250 ml (1 cup) pouring cream
80 g (½ cup) parmesan, grated
salt and pepper
extra shaved parmesan

Cook macaroni in a large saucepan of salted boiling water until *al dente*. Drain.

Heat butter in a large pan and add onion. Cook until soft. Add blanched asparagus and ham and sauté for 2–3 minutes.

Stir in cream and grated parmesan and simmer for 2 minutes or until cream thickens slightly. Season with salt and pepper. Pour sauce over drained pasta, and toss to combine. Serve immediately, topped with extra shaved parmesan.

Serves 4

spaghetti carbonara

This classic Roman dish has many variations and origins. My recipe was inspired by cooking teacher Biba Caggiano, who teaches northern Italian dishes with great enthusiasm and expertise.

The sauce is so quick and easy it can be made while the water is coming to the boil for the pasta.

500 g (1 lb) spaghetti
1 tablespoon olive oil
200 g (7 oz) pancetta, diced
2 eggs
125 ml (½ cup) pouring cream
80 g (½ cup) Parmigiano-Reggiano, grated
cracked black pepper

Cook pasta in a large saucepan of salted boiling water until *al dente*. Drain.

Heat olive oil in a pan and cook pancetta over low heat until crisp. Beat eggs and cream in a bowl with Parmigiano-Reggiano. Add mixture to the drained pasta (it must still be hot so the sauce will be warmed through) and stir quickly to coat with the cream sauce. Add pancetta and toss well.

Serve with plenty of freshly ground black pepper.

Serves 4

with parmesan

linguine with
chicken livers

500 g (1 lb) linguine
2 tablespoons olive oil
2 onions, finely sliced
250 g (8 oz) chicken livers, trimmed and chopped
1 tablespoon chopped sage leaves
250 ml (1 cup) pouring cream
2 eggs, beaten
salt and black pepper
2 tablespoons parmesan, grated

Cook pasta in a large saucepan of salted boiling water until *al dente*. Drain.

Place olive oil in a pan over medium heat and add onions, stirring until golden. Add chicken livers and cook gently for 2–3 minutes or until they just change colour. Stir in sage and cream and cook over low heat for 2–3 minutes. Add eggs and stir quickly to combine. Remove from heat and season with salt and black pepper. Pour sauce over drained pasta, toss gently and serve sprinkled with parmesan.

Serves 4

pad thai fried noodles

black bean beef on crispy noodles

thai-style crispy fried noodles

chinese stir-fried vegetables with vermicelli

spicy and sour crab

quick chicken and bok choy stir-fry

galangal, chicken and green mango stir-fry

nasi goreng

stir-fried yabbies

king prawns with garlic and rice noodles

gai-lan and barbecued pork stir-fry

vegetarian mee goreng

out
of the
wok

pad thai fried noodles

Carol Selva Rajah is a sincere friend and colleague who is always happy to share her vast knowledge of Asian cuisine. She is a professional chef, teacher and food historian in Sydney and has written many books on the subject.

Dried prawns, which are a bright pinkish-orange, are readily available from Asian food stores.

300 g (10 oz) dried thin rice noodles

60 ml (¼ cup) vegetable oil

2 teaspoons chopped ginger

5 cloves garlic, chopped

300 g (10 oz) medium-sized green (raw) prawns (shrimps), peeled and deveined, tails intact

150 g (5 oz) squid tubes, cleaned, cut into 3 cm (1½ in) pieces and scored in a diamond pattern

2 tablespoons fish sauce

2 tablespoons chilli sauce

2 tablespoons palm sugar

3 eggs, lightly beaten

75 g (1 cup) beansprouts

100 g (3½ oz) snowpeas (mange-tout), topped and tailed

1 tablespoon tomato sauce

5 spring onions (scallions), chopped

50 g (1½ oz) whole dried prawns (shrimps)

3 tablespoons unsalted peanuts, crushed

¼ cup coriander (cilantro) leaves

1 fresh small red chilli, seeded and chopped

2 limes, quartered, for garnish

Soak noodles in cold water for 30 minutes, then drain.

Heat oil in a wok, add ginger and garlic and stir-fry until golden. Add prawns and squid and stir over high heat until prawns are pale pink and squid has curled. Add sauces and sugar and stir over heat until sugar has dissolved. Remove contents from wok.

Add eggs to the same wok and keep the wok moving so the egg distributes well over the base. When the egg begins to set, scramble with a fork.

Return seafood mixture to the wok, add drained noodles, beansprouts, snowpeas and tomato sauce in batches and toss well to heat through. Add spring onions, dried prawns, 2 tablespoons peanuts, coriander and chilli and stir to combine.

Serve immediately, sprinkled with the remaining peanuts and accompanied by lime wedges.

Serves 4

black bean beef
on crispy noodles

400 g (14 oz) thin dried egg noodles

2 teaspoons sesame oil

2 tablespoons vegetable oil

1 tablespoon freshly grated ginger

2 tablespoons black bean paste

400 g (14 oz) rump steak, cut into thin strips

½ red capsicum (bell pepper), cut into
*   1 cm (½ in) pieces*

200 g (7 oz) shiitake mushrooms, rinsed, stems
*   removed and thinly sliced*

150 g (5 oz) snowpeas (mange-tout), trimmed

3 teaspoons cornflour (cornstarch)

80 ml (⅓ cup) water

2 tablespoons coarsely chopped coriander
*   (cilantro) leaves*

Add noodles to a pan of boiling water and boil for about 5 minutes or until cooked. Drain and rinse under cold water and drain well. Toss with sesame oil and spread on a tray and grill (broil) for 8–10 minutes on each side or until crisp and golden.

Heat vegetable oil in a wok and when hot add ginger and black bean paste. Stir-fry until aromatic. Add beef and stir-fry until beef changes colour. Add capsicum and mushrooms and stir-fry until half cooked. Add snowpeas and stir 1–2 minutes. Mix cornflour with water and stir into wok to thicken sauce.

Serve beef topped with coriander leaves and accompanied by crispy noodles.

Serves 4

thai-style crispy fried noodles

On a return trip to the Oriental Cooking School in Bangkok, San Gajaseni cooked a delicious *mee grob*.

Tao jiaw (preserved salted soya beans) were included in this recipe but I prefer to omit them. Often served with extra chilli on the side in Thailand, the balance of sweet and sour is paramount in this dish.

vegetable oil for frying
100 g (3½ oz) rice vermicelli
150 g (5 oz) firm tofu, cut into 1 cm (½ in) pieces
1 egg, beaten with 1 tablespoon water
1 chicken breast fillet, finely chopped or 250 g (8 oz) minced (ground) chicken
150 g (5 oz) prawn (shrimp) meat, chopped
4 spring onions (scallions), sliced
1 clove garlic, finely chopped
1 tablespoon grated fresh ginger
1½ tablespoons fish sauce
2 tablespoons lemon juice
1½ tablespoons palm sugar
1 tablespoon soya sauce
1 tablespoon tomato sauce
2 small fresh red chillies, chopped or to taste
½ cup coriander (cilantro) leaves

Heat oil in a wok or large pan and fry vermicelli in batches until crisp and puffed. Drain on absorbent paper. Add tofu to wok and cook for 1–2 minutes or until crisp and golden. Drain well.

Pour all but 1 tablespoon of oil from wok and add egg. Cook until egg is set and firm. Remove and chop coarsely. Add 1 tablespoon of oil to wok and add chicken, prawn meat, spring onions, garlic and ginger and stir-fry for 2–3 minutes or until chicken is just cooked.

Add fish sauce, lemon juice, palm sugar, soya sauce, tomato sauce and chillies to taste. Stir well. Combine chicken mixture with noodles and serve topped with coriander leaves.

Serves 4

chinese stir-fried vegetables with vermicelli

This recipe is very versatile; practically any vegetable from the fridge can replace the ones listed here.

vegetable oil for frying

100 g (3½ oz) rice vermicelli

1 teaspoon sesame oil

1 clove garlic, finely chopped

1 tablespoon grated fresh ginger

1 small red capsicum (bell pepper), cut into
  2 cm (¾ in) pieces

1 small green capsicum (bell pepper), cut into 2 cm
  (¾ in) pieces

1 carrot, peeled and thinly sliced

100 g (3½ oz) mushrooms, thinly sliced

100 g (3½ oz) snowpeas (mange-tout), trimmed

6 spring onions (scallions), cut into 4 cm (1½ in) lengths

3 heads bok choy, coarsely chopped

100 g (½ cup) canned bamboo shoots

185 ml (¾ cup) chicken stock

2 tablespoons soya sauce

1 teaspoon oyster sauce

110 g (1½ cups) beansprouts

3 teaspoons cornflour (cornstarch),
  mixed with 2 tablespoons water

Heat oil in wok or large pan and deep-fry vermicelli in batches until crisp and puffed. Drain on absorbent paper.

Drain all but 2 tablespoons oil from wok and add sesame oil. Add garlic and ginger and stir over low heat until aromatic. Add red and green capsicums and carrot and stir-fry over high heat for about 3 minutes. Add mushrooms, snowpeas, spring onions, and bok choy and stir-fry for another 2 minutes or until bok choy is wilted. Add bamboo shoots, chicken stock, soya sauce, oyster sauce and beansprouts and stir. Pour in cornflour mixture and stir until sauce thickens. Remove and serve on top of crisp vermicelli.

Serves 4

spicy and sour crab

Nonya cooking is a delicious blend of Chinese and indigenous Malay styles. This nonya recipe comes from chef Carol Selva Rajah and looked so spectacular that it appeared on the cover of *Australian Gourmet Traveller* magazine.

5 red onions
10 shallots
10 cloves garlic
3 cm (1½ in) piece ginger, peeled and grated
2 stalks lemongrass, chopped
1 tablespoon sambal oelek (see glossary)
1 kg (2 lb) crabs
60 ml (¼ cup) shaohsing (Chinese rice wine)
60 ml (¼ cup) vegetable oil
60 ml (¼ cup) thick Chinese rice vinegar
2 tablespoons kecap manis (see glossary)
250 ml (1 cup) water
caster (superfine) sugar to taste
salt
*garlic chives and sliced spring onions (scallions),
   for garnish*

Process red onions, shallots, garlic, ginger, lemongrass and sambal oelek in food processor until well combined.

Clean crabs, removing carapace and soft tissue to leave meat exposed, and scrub the shells clean. Chop the bodies in half and crack the claws slightly.

Heat wok until hot. Add half the rice wine and swirl gently for 2 minutes over high heat to coat surface.

Pour off wine, add oil to pan and heat until hot. Add the onion paste and stir-fry until aromatic and golden. Add the crabs, remaining wine, vinegar, kecap manis, water, sugar and salt to taste and quickly bring to the boil. Cook over high heat until crabs change colour. Reduce heat and simmer for about 8 minutes, or until sauce reduces a little.

Serve garnished with garlic chives and spring onions and accompanied by steamed rice.

Serves 4

out of the wok

quick chicken
and bok choy stir-fry

300 g (10 oz) dried egg noodles

2 tablespoons peanut oil

2 cloves garlic, finely chopped

2 teaspoons freshly grated ginger

2 chicken breast fillets (about 240 g/8 oz each),
   cut into thin strips

leaves from 3 heads bok choy

3 tablespoons soya sauce

1 tablespoon oyster sauce

1 red chilli, finely sliced or to taste

120 g (½ cup) toasted whole cashew nuts

4 spring onions (scallions), thinly sliced

Cook noodles in plenty of boiling water for
4–5 minutes. Drain and rinse under cold water.
Drain well.

Heat peanut oil in wok and add garlic and ginger.
Stir-fry until aromatic. Add chicken and stir-fry until
chicken changes colour. Add bok choy and stir-fry
until wilted. Add soya sauce, oyster sauce and chilli
and stir to coat chicken and bok choy.

Serve chicken topped with cashew nuts and spring
onions and accompanied by noodles.

Serves 4

galangal, chicken and green mango stir-fry

Galangal is a member of the ginger family and used extensively in Asian cooking. It is also called kha, lesser ginger and laos. This cream-coloured rhizome has pink markings and as it matures the spicy ginger flavour becomes more pungent.

200 g (7 oz) dried wheat noodles
2 cm (¾ in) piece galangal or ginger, peeled
1 clove garlic
6 green peppercorns
4 coriander (cilantro) roots
2 fresh red chillies or to taste
4 chicken breast fillets
2 tablespoons light olive oil
1 red capsicum (bell pepper), sliced
6 spring onions (scallions), sliced
1 small green mango, peeled and sliced
½ cup mint leaves

Dressing
1 teaspoon palm sugar
1 tablespoon soya sauce
2 teaspoons light olive oil
1 teaspoon fish sauce
2 teaspoons mirin (see glossary)
1½ tablespoons lime juice

Cook dried noodles in boiling water for 3–5 minutes or until soft and separated. Drain.

Place galangal, garlic, peppercorns, coriander roots and chillies in a food processor and process until finely chopped. Rub the mixture on the chicken fillets, cover and refrigerate for 30 minutes. Cut chicken into thin strips.

Heat 1 tablespoon oil in a wok and pan-fry the chicken over medium heat until cooked. Remove chicken and rest in a warm place. Add remaining tablespoon of oil and stir-fry capsicum until soft. Add spring onions and mango and stir-fry over low heat until vegetables are heated through.

To make dressing, combine all ingredients in a small bowl and stir until well combined. Place noodles in 4 bowls and add sliced chicken. Top with vegetables and pour dressing over before serving. Garnish with mint leaves.

Serves 4

nasi goreng

This is a very flavoursome Indonesian dish.
Make sure the rice is cold before adding it to
the wok or it will stick.

6 tablespoons vegetable oil

2 eggs, beaten with a little salt

200 g (7 oz) rump steak, thinly sliced

200 g (7 oz) small green (raw) prawns (shrimps),
   shelled and deveined

1 onion, chopped

1 carrot, thinly sliced

1 capsicum (bell pepper), cut into 3 cm (1 in) pieces

2 cloves garlic, finely chopped

2–3 fresh red chillies, finely chopped or to taste

1 tablespoon freshly grated ginger

3 cups cold cooked rice

2 tablespoons kecap manis (see glossary)

4 spring onions (scallions), sliced diagonally

Heat 1 tablespoon of oil in a wok, add eggs and
cook until set and firm. Remove and set aside.

Add another tablespoon of oil and stir-fry beef and
prawns over high heat until they change colour.
Remove and set aside.

Add 2 tablespoons of oil to wok and when hot
add onion, carrot and capsicum and stir-fry for
2–3 minutes. Remove and set aside.

Add remaining oil to wok and stir-fry garlic, chillies
and ginger until aromatic. Add rice and stir-fry
until heated through. Add beef, prawns and
vegetables to rice and stir until heated through.
Sprinkle with kecap manis and stir.

Roll egg up and cut into fine strips. Serve rice
topped with egg and spring onions.

Serves 4–6

stir-fried yabbies

Freshwater yabbies are the smallest species in the freshwater crayfish family and are farmed in many areas of Australia. They are available all year round, but king prawns can be substituted and make an equally tasty dish. Try serving them with a bowl of steamed rice.

3 tablespoons vegetable oil
1½ kg (3 lb) whole green (raw) yabbies, unshelled
4 spring onions (scallions), finely sliced
1 tablespoon finely chopped fresh ginger
¼ cup palm sugar
125 ml (½ cup) chicken stock
sliced fresh red chilli to taste
salt to taste
Thai basil leaves

Heat vegetable oil in wok and when hot add the yabbies (whole) and stir-fry over medium heat until yabbies change colour and are cooked. Remove from wok.

Add spring onions and ginger and stir over low heat until aromatic. Add palm sugar, chicken stock, chilli and salt to taste. Reduce heat, return yabbies to wok and stir to coat with sauce.

Serve yabbies topped with basil leaves and accompanied by steamed rice. Provide finger bowls.

Serves 4 as an entrée

king prawns with
garlic and rice noodles

This irresistible prawn and noodle dish comes
from Australian chef, Richard Purdue.

2½ tablespoons peanut oil

16 large green (raw) prawns (shrimps),
  shelled and deveined, tails intact

8 cloves garlic, finely chopped

4 red chillies, seeded and sliced

leaves from 3 heads bok choy

100 ml (5 tablespoons) oyster sauce

100 ml (5 tablespoons) chicken stock

10 ml (2 teaspoons) sesame oil

200 g (7 oz) fresh rice noodles, soaked briefly
in warm water

Heat oil in wok and stir-fry prawns until just
cooked. Remove prawns, add garlic and chilli.
When garlic starts to colour, add bok choy and
stir until wilted.

Add oyster sauce, stock and sesame oil and stir to
combine. Add drained rice noodles and prawns
and stir to heat through before serving.

Serves 4 as an entrée

out of the wok

gai-lan and barbecued pork stir-fry

Gai-lan is also known as Chinese broccoli. If unavailable, use bok choy.

Barbecued pork (*char siew*) can be purchased from Chinese barbecue shops.

1 tablespoon peanut oil
3 cloves garlic, finely chopped
2 teaspoons finely chopped fresh ginger
2–3 fresh red chillies, finely chopped or to taste
1 bunch gai-lan, cut into 4 cm (2½ in) lengths
125 ml (½ cup) chicken stock
500 g (1 lb) barbecued pork, sliced
2 tablespoons oyster sauce, mixed with
  1 tablespoon water

Heat oil in wok and when hot add garlic, ginger and chillies and stir-fry until fragrant.

Add *gai-lan* stems and stir 1–2 minutes, add *gai-lan* leaves and chicken stock, cover and cook for 2–3 minutes.

Add pork and stir until heated through. Remove from heat and drizzle with oyster sauce. Serve with cooked wheat noodles or steamed jasmine rice.

Serves 4

vegetarian

mee goreng

Scotts Road in Singapore is a beehive of activity day and night and the Hyatt Regency Hotel is situated amidst all the colour and excitement. The chefs in the hotel restaurants create some of the best authentic dishes available in Singapore. Vegetarian *mee goreng* is just one of them and very easy to make.

   Ready-fried crisp shallots are available from Asian food stores.

400 g Hokkien noodles
2 tablespoons vegetable oil
3 cloves garlic, finely chopped
1 small onion, finely sliced
1½ cups (about 110 g) beansprouts
½ bunch choy sum, trimmed
1 small tomato, chopped
1 small desirée potato, chopped and blanched
   in boiling water for 2 minutes
2 teaspoons sambal oelek (see glossary), or to taste
60 ml (¼ cup) tomato sauce
1 tablespoon light soya sauce
2 teaspoons dark soya sauce
2 teaspoons fried shallots
1 lime, cut into wedges

Place noodles in a heatproof bowl and cover with boiling water for 30 seconds. Drain well.

Heat oil in a wok, add garlic and onion and cook for 30 seconds. Add vegetables, sambal oelek and sauces and cook, stirring for 2–3 minutes, or until choy sum is wilted. Add noodles and stir until heated through.

Serve sprinkled with fried shallots and accompanied by lime wedges.

Serves 2–3

green lasagne with basil and peas

baked eggplant with zucchini and fontina

pasta roll with spinach filling

semolina gnocchi

joanne weir's creamy garlic 'risotto' with prawns

cannelloni of asparagus

crêpes stuffed with tomato, ham and cheese

mushroom and capsicum lasagne

baked pasta with asparagus and artichokes

nan's lemon chicken

hot from the oven

green lasagne with basil and peas

This lasagne can be made with green or white pasta and a layer of sliced sautéed eggplant in the centre makes an interesting variation.

Béchamel Sauce
4 tablespoons unsalted butter
3 tablespoons plain (all-purpose) flour
500 ml (2 cups) milk, hot
salt and black pepper

250 g (8 oz) dried lasagne sheets
500 ml (2 cups) tomato sauce (see page 3 for recipe)
1½ cups fresh green peas, blanched
200 g (7 oz) ham, shredded
300 g (10 oz) bocconcini, coarsely grated
20 basil leaves, roughly torn
salt and black pepper
80 g (½ cup) parmesan, grated
2 tablespoons butter

Cook lasagne sheets in a large saucepan of salted boiling water until *al dente*. Drain.

To make the béchamel sauce, melt butter over low heat and add flour, stirring to combine. Add milk and stir continuously over low heat until the sauce thickens and coats the back of a spoon. Season with salt and pepper and cover until needed.

Preheat the oven to 180°C (350°F).

Spread 2 tablespoons tomato sauce over the base of a shallow ovenproof dish (20 cm x 30 cm/8 in x 12 in). Place one-third of the lasagne sheets on top of the sauce. Spread one-third of the béchamel sauce over the pasta, then half the peas, half the tomato sauce, half the ham and one-third of the bocconcini. Scatter with 10 basil leaves and season with salt and pepper. Sprinkle with about 1 tablespoon parmesan.

Top with another third of the lasagne sheets and spread with one-third of the béchamel, then remaining peas, tomato sauce and one-third of the bocconcini. Scatter with remaining basil leaves, season with salt and pepper and sprinkle with about 1 tablespoon parmesan. Cover with remaining lasagne sheets and spread with remaining béchamel, bocconcini and sprinkle with parmesan. Dot with butter and bake for 25–30 minutes or until top is golden. Rest 5 minutes before serving.

Serves 4–6

baked eggplant
with zucchini and fontina

This dish is typical of southern Italy and delicious hot or cold served with crusty bread.

2 medium-sized eggplants (aubergines),
*   sliced 1 cm (½ in) thick*
salt and black pepper
250 ml (1 cup) olive oil
4 zucchinis (courgettes), sliced lengthways
*   into 1 cm (½ in) thick slices*
1 cup tomato passata (see glossary)
100 g (1 cup) fontina, coarsely grated
120 g (¾ cup) parmesan, grated
3 tablespoons chopped fresh oregano
8 kalamata olives, pitted and sliced

Salt eggplant for about 20 minutes. Rinse and pat dry.

Heat oil in a large pan and fry eggplant until golden on both sides. Drain on paper towels. Fry zucchini slices on both sides and drain well.

Preheat the oven to 180°C (350°F).

Smear the base of a 28 cm x 18 cm (11 in x 7 in) shallow ovenproof dish with 3 tablespoons of the tomato passata and top with a layer of eggplant and a third of the zucchini slices. Drizzle with tomato passata and a third of the fontina cheese, 1 tablespoon of parmesan and 1 tablespoon of oregano. Season with salt and pepper. Repeat with a second and third layer, finishing with the remaining tomato passata and sprinkle with the remaining cheeses. Add olives and bake for 20–25 minutes or until golden.

Serves 4

pasta roll with spinach filling

My first authentic Italian cooking lesson was in Bologna with Marcella Hazan. During the first lesson there was a little chatter from the class as students from different countries became acquainted but that ceased abruptly when Marcella blew the large silver whistle around her neck at full blast!

The following recipe for *rotolo di pasta* is a variation of Marcella's superb dish.

500 g (1 lb) frozen spinach, thawed

100 g (½ cup) butter

salt and pepper to taste

1 small brown onion, finely chopped

4 slices (about 60 g/2 oz) prosciutto, finely chopped

200 g (7 oz) ricotta cheese, drained and crumbled

80 g (½ cup) Parmigiano-Reggiano, grated

¼ teaspoon freshly grated nutmeg

1 egg yolk

2 fresh lasagne sheets, each measuring approximately 30 cm x 20 cm (12 in x 8 in)

250 ml (1 cup) tomato sauce (see page 3 for recipe)

extra shaved Parmigiano-Reggiano

Cook spinach with 20 g (1 tablespoon) of the butter, salt and pepper over low heat for about 5 minutes. Set aside. Sauté onion with 50 g (4 tablespoons) butter over medium heat until golden and then add prosciutto and stir for 2 minutes. Add spinach and cook, stirring for 2–3 minutes.

Transfer spinach mixture to a large bowl and add ricotta, grated Parmigiano-Reggiano, nutmeg, and egg yolk. Mix with a fork until well combined. Add salt and pepper to taste. Spread half the mixture over one pasta sheet, leaving a border about 2 cm (¾ in). Fold the pasta sheet and continue to fold until it is rolled up. Repeat with remaining sheet. Wrap the rolls in muslin or a clean tea-towel and tie the ends securely with kitchen string. Then tie the roll two or three times at evenly spaced intervals.

Bring 3–4 litres (6–8 pints) water to the boil in a large saucepan and add 2 teaspoons of salt. Place pasta rolls in water and bring back to a steady boil. Simmer for 15–20 minutes. Remove rolls carefully with slotted spoons.

Heat tomato sauce in a pan. When pasta rolls have cooled a little remove muslin and cut into slices about 3 cm (1 in) thick. Pour hot tomato sauce onto 4 serving plates and arrange pasta slices on top of sauce. Top with extra shaved Parmigiano-Reggiano. The rolls can be made ahead, covered and refrigerated.

Serves 4

semolina gnocchi

My family and I enjoyed Valentina Harris's semolina gnocchi after a very exciting truffle hunt in Alba, Piedmont and it has remained a favourite. Valentina is well known for her BBC television series on Italian regional cookery and now conducts very popular cooking schools in Piedmont and other regions of Italy at different seasons of the year. Cinnamon or nutmeg can be used to spice my variation of her fabulous dish.

1 litre (4 cups) milk
250 g (2 cups) semolina
1 egg
100 g (1¼ cups) parmesan, grated
50 g (¼ cup) butter
a pinch of nutmeg
salt and black pepper

Bring milk to the boil in a large saucepan, reduce heat and add semolina gradually, whisking constantly to prevent lumps. Cook uncovered, stirring frequently, over low heat for 7–10 minutes or until mixture comes away from the sides of the pan easily. Remove from heat and stir in egg, half the parmesan and half the butter, nutmeg, salt and pepper. Spread mixture onto a lightly oiled oven tray and smooth with a wet knife to a thickness of about 1 cm (½ in). Rest, covered in the refrigerator, until firm.

Preheat the oven to 200°C (400°F).

Cut semolina into circles using a 4 cm (1½ in) pastry cutter. Arrange a layer of the gnocchi in a greased shallow ovenproof dish. Dot with remaining butter and sprinkle with the remaining parmesan. Bake for about 15 minutes or until golden.

Serves 4–6

joanne weir's creamy garlic 'risotto' with prawns

Garlic mayonnaise

2 cloves garlic, finely chopped

1 cup mayonnaise

6 tablespoons olive oil

2 medium-sized onions, chopped

a large pinch of saffron

5 tomatoes, chopped, or 2 cups canned tomatoes,
drained and chopped

4 cloves garlic, finely chopped

a large pinch of cayenne

1 teaspoon paprika

1 tablespoon chopped flat-leaf (Italian) parsley

1 bay leaf

a pinch of dried thyme

125 ml (½ cup) dry white wine

1.5 kg (3 lb) fish bones, trimmed and washed

1.5 litres (3 pints) water

salt and black pepper

350 g (12 oz) spaghetti, broken into
2 cm (¾ in) lengths

750 g (1½ lb) green (raw) king prawns (large shrimps),
shelled and deveined

To make the garlic mayonnaise, combine the chopped garlic and mayonnaise and stir well.

In a large pan heat 2 tablespoons of oil and add onions. Sauté over low heat for about 30 minutes uncovered, stirring occasionally, until onions just begin to turn golden.

Heat the saffron in a small pan over medium heat, shaking frequently, for 1 minute. Add the saffron, tomatoes, garlic, cayenne, paprika and parsley to the onions and continue to cook, uncovered, for 10 minutes. Remove from the heat and purée in a blender until smooth. Transfer to a stock pot. Add bay leaf, thyme, wine, fish bones and water. Bring to the boil and simmer slowly, uncovered, for 35 minutes. Strain the stock and season with salt and pepper.

Preheat the oven to 220°C (425°F).

Heat 4 tablespoons olive oil in a shallow pan until very hot. Remove from heat and add pasta, salt and pepper and mix well. Return to the heat and stirring constantly, cook pasta uncovered for about 3 minutes or until a light golden brown.

Heat fish stock to a low simmer and gradually add to the pasta, one cup at a time, allowing pasta to absorb stock after each addition. Add as much stock as needed until the pasta is almost cooked, about 10 minutes. Add the last cup of stock and the prawns and continue to cook for about 5 minutes or until pasta is tender and very moist. Add a little extra water if necessary.

Bake for 5–7 minutes until pasta is crispy on top but moist underneath. Serve accompanied by a bowl of garlic mayonnaise.

Serves 6

hot from the oven

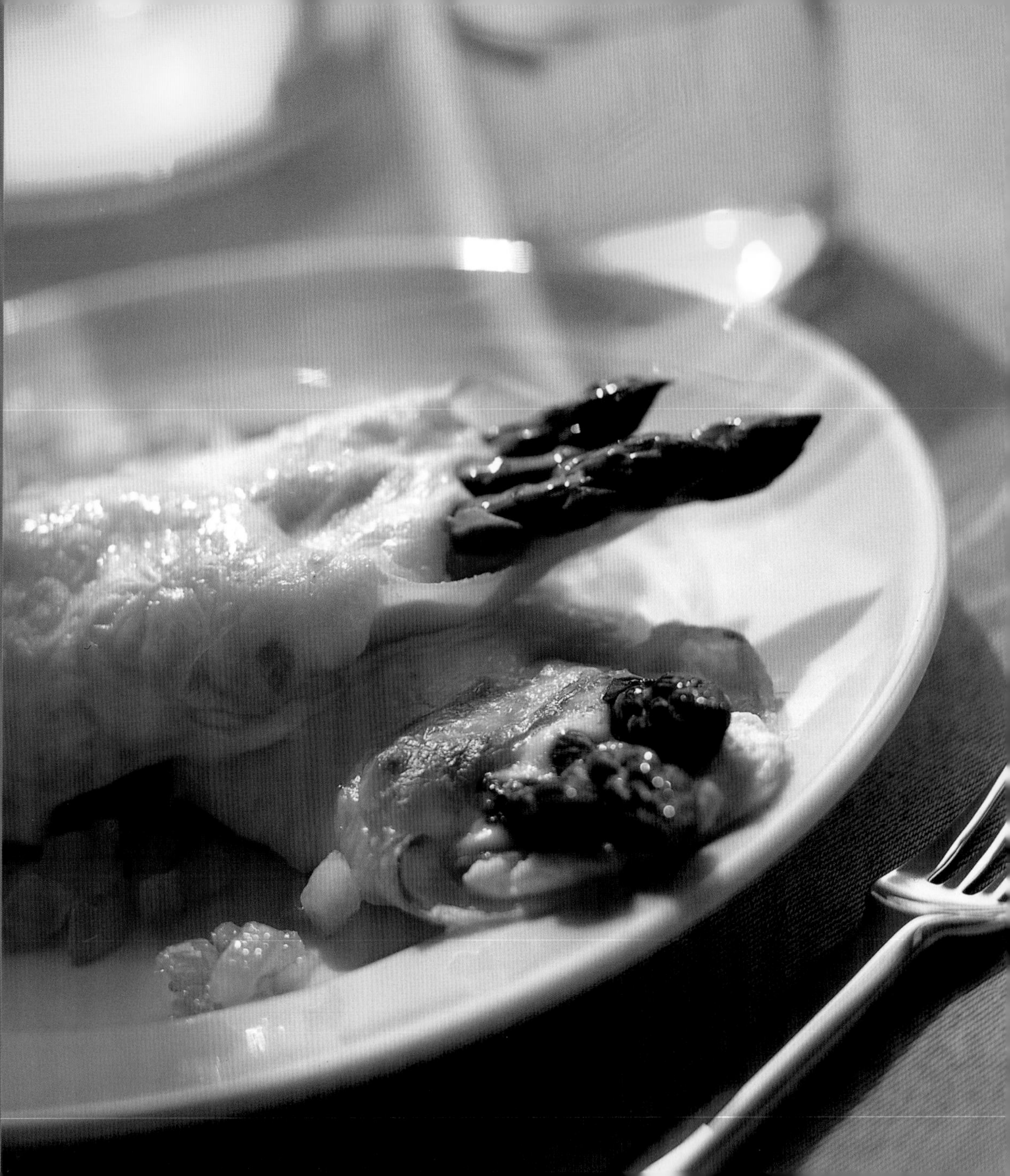

cannelloni
of asparagus

This recipe comes from Alex Herbert, one of Sydney's innovative chefs. Try it in the spring when green, white and purple asparagus are in season.

   Verjuice is partially fermented grape juice. If it's unavailable, use dry white wine instead.

6 fresh pasta squares, approximately
   15 cm (6 in) square
450 g (15 oz) fresh ricotta
12 thin slices prosciutto
18 green asparagus spears, trimmed and simmered in
   lightly salted water for 5 minutes and then drained
salt and pepper
2 white onions, thinly sliced
100 ml (scant ½ cup) olive oil
100 ml (scant ½ cup) verjuice
300 g (10 oz) bocconcini, sliced

Lay out pasta sheets and spread about 75 g (5 tablespoons) ricotta on each. Top each square with 2 slices of prosciutto. Place 3 asparagus spears on each sheet, season with salt and pepper and roll up.

Preheat the oven to 180°C (350°F).

Sauté onion in olive oil over medium heat for 8–10 minutes or until translucent. Add verjuice, salt and pepper and cook over medium heat until liquid is reduced by half. Remove from heat and set aside.

Place half the onion mixture on a greased baking tray and place the cannelloni on top of onion. Spread remaining onion on top of cannelloni and place sliced mozzarella on top of onion mix to cover pasta. Bake for 15–20 minutes.

Serves 6 as an entrée or 3 as a main course

crêpes stuffed with tomato, ham and cheese

Marcella Hazan described this dish (*tortino di crespelle*) in Bologna and I couldn't wait to get home and try it. It has now become a family favourite served with a green salad on Sunday nights. The crêpes can be made ahead and frozen, which makes the recipe quick and easy to prepare. Shredded ham or prosciutto works equally well.

1 cup tomato sauce (see page 3 for recipe)
200 g (7 oz) ham, shredded
80 g (½ cup) parmesan, grated
50 g (½ cup) fontina, coarsely grated

Crêpes
300 ml (1¼ cups) milk
110 g (⅔ cup) plain (all-purpose) flour
2 large eggs
¼ teaspoon salt
butter for greasing pan

To make the crêpes, whisk milk and flour in a bowl until smooth. Add eggs and salt and beat until well combined. Cover and rest for 15 minutes.

Pour about 2 tablespoons of batter onto a greased heated pan and swirl to coat. Cook crêpes on both sides until light golden in colour. Continue until all the batter is used up.

Preheat the oven to 200°C (400°F).

Place a crêpe on the base of a greased 22 cm (9 in) cake tin with a removable base. Spread about 2 tablespoons tomato sauce over the crêpe. Spread a little of the ham, parmesan, and fontina over the crêpe. Repeat until all the crêpes are used up, finishing with grated parmesan on the top. Bake for 15 minutes. Serve hot or at room temperature, cut into wedges.

Serves 4

mushroom and capsicum lasagne

25 g (1 oz) dried porcini mushrooms
250 g (8 oz) dried lasagne sheets
3 tablespoons olive oil
1 leek, cut into ½ cm (¼ in) thick slices
2 cloves garlic, finely chopped
500 g (1 lb) mushrooms, sliced
1 red capsicum (bell pepper), sliced
1 tablespoon plain (all-purpose) flour
salt and black pepper
250 ml (1 cup) hot chicken stock
2 tablespoons tomato paste
2–3 sprigs thyme
120 g (¾ cup) parmesan, grated
100 g (1 cup) fontina, coarsely grated

Béchamel Sauce
2 tablespoons butter
2 tablespoons plain (all-purpose) flour
500 ml (2 cups) milk

Soak porcini mushrooms in hot water for 15 minutes. Drain and chop.

Cook lasagne sheets in a large pan of salted boiling water until *al dente*. Drain.

Heat olive oil in a pan and add leek. Stir over medium heat for 2 minutes or until wilted. Add garlic, porcini, mushrooms and capsicum and cook for 10 minutes. Add 1 tablespoon of flour and stir for 2 minutes. Season with salt and pepper. Pour in chicken stock, stir and cook for 2 minutes. Add tomato paste and thyme leaves and stir well to combine. Set aside.

Preheat the oven to 180°C (350°F).

To make the béchamel sauce, melt butter in a pan over medium heat and add flour. Stir for 2 minutes and remove from heat. Stir in milk until smooth. Return to heat and cook, stirring, until the sauce thickens.

Smear the base of a 20 cm x 30 cm (8 in x 12 in) shallow ovenproof dish with a little of the sauce and cover with one-third of the lasagne sheets. Top with half of the mushroom mixture and one-third of the béchamel sauce and about 2 tablespoons of parmesan. Cover with another third of the lasagne sheets and top with remaining mushroom mixture and another third of the béchamel sauce and about 2 tablespoons of parmesan. Finish with remaining lasagne sheets and spread with remaining béchamel sauce and fontina cheese. Sprinkle with remaining parmesan and bake for 25–30 minutes or until golden. Rest for 5 minutes before serving.

Serves 6

baked pasta with
asparagus and artichokes

500 g (1 lb) fusilli (spiral-shaped) pasta

2 bunches green asparagus (about 400 g/14 oz),
   trimmed and cut into 2 cm (¾ in) lengths

6 tablespoons butter

2 tablespoons plain (all-purpose) flour

500 ml (2 cups) milk

250 ml (1 cup) chicken stock

salt and pepper

¼ teaspoon ground cinnamon

300 g (10 oz) ricotta, crumbled

200 g (7 oz) artichokes in oil, drained and sliced

120 g (¾ cup) parmesan, grated

Cook pasta in a large saucepan of salted boiling water until half cooked. Add asparagus and continue to cook until pasta is *al dente*. Drain. Toss with 2 tablespoons of the butter.

Preheat the oven to 180°C (350°F).

Heat another 2 tablespoons butter in a pan over medium heat and when melted add flour and stir for 2 minutes. Remove from heat, stir in milk and chicken stock. Return to the heat and stir for about 3 minutes or until mixture thickens. Season with salt, pepper and cinnamon. Combine pasta with sauce and stir in ricotta, artichokes, and half the parmesan.

Pour into a large lightly greased ovenproof dish and sprinkle with remaining parmesan. Dot with remaining butter. Bake for 15–18 minutes or until golden and crisp on top.

Serves 6

nan's lemon chicken

This delicious recipe comes from a great
American cook and dear friend, Nancy Pilcher.
Quick to whip up, it is great for a crowd and
can be kept, covered, in the oven if necessary.

75 g (½ cup) plain (all-purpose) flour
½ teaspoon paprika
salt and cracked black pepper
4 chicken half-breasts (with bone and skin attached)
125 ml (½ cup) vegetable oil
finely grated rind of 2 lemons
juice of 2 lemons
1 clove garlic, finely chopped
2 tablespoons soya sauce

Preheat the oven to 200°C (400°F).

Place flour, paprika, salt and pepper in a large
plastic bag. Add chicken pieces and shake to coat
with the flour mixture. Remove chicken and shake
off excess flour.

In a medium-sized bowl mix vegetable oil with
rind and juice of the lemons, garlic and soya sauce.
Whisk until well combined.

Place chicken, skin side down, in a shallow
ovenproof dish. Pour lemon mixture evenly over
chicken. Bake covered for 30 minutes. Remove
cover, turn chicken pieces over and continue to
bake uncovered for another 20 minutes or until
golden and cooked.

Serves 4

farfalle with grilled chicken, herb and lemon salad

linguine with spring vegetables

orecchiette with roasted red and yellow capsicum

spinach and ricotta gnocchi

conchiglie with basil, lemon and ricotta

pappardelle with rocket, chervil, eggplant and roasted garlic

orecchiette with tomato and rocket

orzo with zucchini flowers and cream

spicy chicken in radicchio cups

trenette with pesto

tagliatelle with lemon butter sauce

fresh from the garden

farfalle with grilled chicken, herb and lemon salad

Californian chef Joanne Weir is often described as a minute, dark-haired tornado in the kitchen. She visits Australia regularly, and her vibrant personality and vast knowledge of Mediterranean and Californian cuisine ensure that her cooking classes are booked out many months ahead. Her first splendid book, *From Tapas to Meze*, concentrates on first courses and contains many updated versions of traditional Mediterranean and Californian recipes. This tasty recipe was inspired by one of her trips to Morocco.

80 ml (⅓ cup) extra-virgin olive oil
3 tablespoons lemon juice
3 cloves garlic, finely chopped
¾ teaspoon ground cumin
salt and freshly ground pepper
3 x 250 g (8 oz) boned chicken breasts, trimmed
1 tablespoon extra-virgin olive oil

1.25 litres (5 cups) rich homemade chicken stock
300 g (10 oz) farfalle (bow-shaped) pasta
½ cup flat-leaf (Italian) parsley leaves
¾ cup coriander (cilantro) leaves
¾ cup basil leaves, torn into large pieces
½ cup mint leaves
½ cups rocket (arugula) leaves
1 preserved lemon, finely chopped

In a large bowl whisk together 80 ml (⅓ cup) olive oil, lemon juice, garlic, cumin, salt and pepper. Set aside.

Heat a cast-iron grill over medium heat for about 10 minutes. Brush chicken breasts with a tablespoon of olive oil. Cook the chicken on the grill until golden on one side, 3–4 minutes. Turn the chicken over, season with salt and pepper and continue to cook until done, 4–5 minutes. Slice the chicken into thin strips. Reserve.

Place the chicken stock in a saucepan and reduce by half over medium heat. Add the oil/lemon juice mixture and reserve. Cook pasta in plenty of salted boiling water for 10–12 minutes or until *al dente*. Drain the pasta and toss immediately in the oil/lemon juice mixture, add chicken pieces, parsley, coriander, basil, mint, rocket, preserved lemon, and salt and pepper to taste. Toss well, place on a platter and serve immediately.

Serves 6

linguine with
spring vegetables

Linguine is a flat narrow ribbon pasta.

500 g (1 lb) linguine
400 g (14 oz) fresh peas, shelled
1 small zucchini (courgette), finely sliced
1 bunch asparagus, trimmed and cut into
  1 cm (1/2 in) lengths
200 g (7 oz) fresh broad (fava) beans
1 tablespoon butter
100 g (3 1/2 oz) small mushrooms, sliced
salt and black pepper
250 ml (1 cup) pouring cream
80 g (1/2 cup) parmesan, grated
12 basil leaves, roughly torn

Cook pasta in a large pan of salted boiling water until *al dente*. Drain.

Cook peas, zucchini, asparagus and broad beans in lightly salted water until tender but still crisp. Drain.

Melt butter in a large pan and sauté mushrooms until soft. Add drained vegetables, salt, plenty of cracked black pepper and cream to the mushrooms and stir for 2 minutes over low heat. Toss pasta with vegetables and parmesan and serve topped with torn basil leaves.

Serves 4

orrechiette with roasted red and yellow capsicum

500 g (1 lb) orrechiette (ear-shaped) pasta

2 tablespoons extra-virgin olive oil

3 cloves garlic, finely chopped

1 onion, sliced

2 red capsicums (bell peppers), roasted and peeled

2 yellow capsicums (bell peppers), roasted and peeled

100 g (about 4 cups) rocket (arugula) leaves,
*   coarsely chopped*

salt and cracked black pepper

3 tablespoons parmesan, grated

Cook pasta in plenty of salted boiling water until *al dente*. Drain.

Heat oil in a small pan and add garlic and onion. Stir over low heat until onion is soft. Cut capsicums into strips. Pour pasta into a large serving dish and add onion mixture, capsicums and rocket leaves. Toss to combine. Season to taste with salt and pepper. Serve topped with grated parmesan.

Serves 4

fresh from the garden

spinach and ricotta gnocchi

It is important to work the mixture for gnocchi very lightly and not overcook it or the dumplings will be tough.

100 g (½ cup) butter
500 g (1 lb) frozen spinach, thawed and drained
500 g (1 lb) ricotta, well drained
2 large eggs, lightly beaten
120 g (¾ cup) parmesan, grated
salt and black pepper
a pinch of nutmeg
150 g (1 cup) plain (all-purpose) flour

Melt 2 tablespoons of the butter in a pan over medium heat, add spinach and stir for about 5 minutes or until moisture is absorbed. Remove and chop.

In a large pan combine spinach, ricotta, eggs, half the parmesan, salt, pepper and nutmeg. Mix in 2–3 tablespoons flour to thicken mixture. Shape tablespoons of the mixture into croquettes (small oval shapes of about 3 cm x 6 cm [1½ in x 2½ in]) and dust lightly with flour.

Bring a large pan of salted water to the boil and cook gnocchi, a few at a time, for 2–4 minutes or until they float to the surface. Remove with a slotted spoon and place in a lightly greased ovenproof dish. Melt remaining butter and pour over gnocchi. Top with remaining parmesan and place under a hot grill until cheese is golden.

Serves 4

conchiglie with basil, lemon and ricotta

Spending a few days in the kitchens at the Grand Hotel Cocumella, Sorrento, with Rosa Russo was one of the highlights of a trip to southern Italy. This ancient hotel, perched high on the cliff overlooking the aqua sea across to Naples, was once a monastery and is quite unique with its two very contrasting kitchens. The regular commercial kitchen serves the main areas, and the second, a home-style kitchen, is the domain of Russo who cooks for the Scintilla Restaurant. She taught me many traditional dishes that have been passed on through her family. Several recipes included lemon zest, juice or leaves from large thick-skinned lemons with excellent flavour. Here is my version of her pasta with lemon and ricotta.

400 g (14 oz) conchiglie (shell-shaped) pasta
zest of 1½ lemons
1 cup basil leaves, roughly torn
250 g (8 oz) fresh ricotta, crumbled
2 tablespoons chopped flat-leaf (Italian) parsley
150 ml (⅔ cup) pouring cream
salt and cracked black pepper
50 g (1½ oz) pecorino, finely grated
4 tablespoons extra-virgin olive oil

Cook pasta in plenty of salted boiling water until *al dente*. Drain.

In a large bowl mix lemon zest, basil, ricotta, parsley and cream. Place hot pasta on top of lemon mixture and toss gently to combine. Add salt and plenty of cracked black pepper.

Serve pasta topped with pecorino cheese and drizzled with olive oil.

Serves 4

pappardelle with
rocket, chervil, eggplant and roasted garlic

Pappardelle is a very wide flat ribbon pasta.

4 small, purple eggplants (aubergines)
olive oil for frying
1 tablespoon balsamic vinegar
500 g (1 lb) pappardelle
2 anchovy fillets, finely chopped
100 g (3½ oz) baby rocket (arugula) leaves
4 tablespoons extra-virgin olive oil
12 cloves garlic, roasted until soft and then peeled
salt and black pepper
2 tablespoons fresh chervil leaves

Slice eggplant and fry in olive oil until soft. Drain on absorbent paper and sprinkle with vinegar.

Cook pappardelle in plenty of salted boiling water until *al dente*. Drain. Pour into a large serving bowl and add eggplant, anchovy fillets, rocket, olive oil, garlic, salt and pepper. Toss gently to combine and serve topped with fresh chervil leaves.

Serves 4

orrechiette with
tomato and rocket

This pasta dish is perfect when you're short of time to prepare. Choose small rocket (arugula) leaves, which are tender and not as pepppery as the larger mature leaves.

500 g (1 lb) orrechiette (ear-shaped) pasta
2 tablespoons olive oil
½ onion, finely chopped
2 cloves garlic, finely chopped
400 g (14 oz) plum (Roma) tomatoes,
  peeled and coarsely chopped
salt
dried red chilli flakes to taste
1 bunch rocket (arugula) leaves, coarsely chopped
6 tablespoons extra-virgin olive oil

Cook pasta in a large pan of salted boiling water until *al dente*. Drain.

Heat olive oil in a pan and sauté onion over medium heat until soft. Add garlic and stir until aromatic. Add tomatoes to pan and cook over low heat for about 10 minutes or until thickened. Add salt and chilli flakes. Toss pasta with tomato sauce and rocket leaves. Drizzle with extra-virgin olive oil before serving.

Serves 4

orzo with zucchini flowers and cream

400 g (14 oz) orzo (rice-shaped) pasta
3 tablespoons butter
1 onion, chopped
2 cloves garlic, chopped
4 zucchinis (courgettes), chopped
375 ml (1½ cups) pouring cream
80 g (1½ cups) Parmigiano-Reggiano, grated
12 zucchini (courgette) flowers
salt and black pepper
½ cup small fresh basil leaves

Cook pasta in plenty of salted boiling water until *al dente*. Drain.

Heat butter in a large pan and add onion and garlic. Stir until onion is soft. Add chopped zucchini and cook until just tender. Add cream and cook over medium heat until slightly thickened. Add cheese and zucchini flowers and stir until flowers are wilted. Add zucchini sauce to pasta and toss gently to combine. Season with salt and pepper. Serve topped with small fresh basil leaves.

Serves 4

spicy chicken
in radicchio cups

6 cup-shaped radicchio leaves

25 g (1 oz) bean thread noodles (see glossary)

6 pieces cloud-ear fungus (see glossary)

2 tablespoons peanut oil

1 clove garlic, finely chopped

2 teaspoons ginger, grated

250 g (8 oz) minced (ground) chicken

½ cup water chestnuts, sliced

½ cup bamboo shoots, sliced

2–3 red chillies, finely sliced

3 spring onions (scallions), finely sliced

75 g (1 cup) beansprouts

1 tablespoon shaohsing (Chinese rice wine)

1 tablespoon soya sauce

1 teaspoon oyster sauce

½ teaspoon caster (superfine) sugar

salt and pepper

1 teaspoon cornflour (cornstarch), mixed with
  3 tablespoons water

soya sauce or sweet chilli sauce

Wash radicchio leaves and chill until crisp.

Soak cellophane noodles and cloud-ear fungus in separate bowls in enough hot water to cover Drain noodles after 5 minutes and cut into shorter lengths. Soak fungus for 15 minutes, then drain and cut into fine strips.

Heat peanut oil in wok over medium heat and when hot add garlic and ginger and stir-fry until aromatic. Add chicken and stir until half cooked. Add noodles and fungus and stir until heated through. Add water chestnuts, bamboo shoots and chillies and stir. Add spring onions and beansprouts and stir for 1 minute. Add rice wine, soya sauce, oyster sauce and sugar and stir. Season with salt and pepper. Add cornflour mixture and stir for 1 minute. Remove from heat and serve chicken in chilled radicchio cups accompanied by soya or a sweet chilli sauce.

Serves 6 as an entrée

fresh from the garden

trenette with pesto

In Liguria pesto is traditionally made in
a mortar and pestle and often served
with trenette (ribbon pasta). This sauce
is also delicious on boiled potatoes.
Substitute fettuccine or spaghetti if
trenette is not available.

500 g (1 lb) trenette pasta
leaves from 2 bunches fresh basil
2 tablespoons pinenuts
2 cloves garlic
80 g (½ cup) Parmigiano-Reggiano
2 tablespoons pecorino • Cows milk cheese
200 ml (¾ cup) extra-virgin olive oil
a pinch of rock salt
cracked black pepper
extra grated Parmigiano-Reggiano

2 oz

Also Delia Smith -
Summer Collection
Page 35

Cook pasta in plenty of salted boiling water. Drain,
reserving 3 tablespoons of the pasta water.

Place basil, pinenuts, garlic, Parmigiano-Reggiano
and pecorino in a food processor and process until
combined. Add oil in a steady stream with the
motor running and process until smooth. Season
with salt and pepper. Stir reserved pasta water into
pesto. Toss pesto with pasta and top with extra
grated cheese.

Serves 4

tagliatelle with
lemon butter sauce

This quick flavoursome recipe is from Carla Tomasi of Tasting Places in Menfi, where many dishes contain the tangy flavour of the lemons that grow in abundance in Sicily.

500 g (1 lb) fresh tagliatelle
250 g (8 oz) unsalted butter, softened
juice of 4 large lemons
finely grated zest of 4 large lemons
salt and plenty of cracked black pepper
50 g (1½ oz) pecorino, finely grated

Cook pasta in plenty of salted boiling water until *al dente*. Drain.

Cut butter into small pieces and process in a food processor until pale and fluffy. With the motor running, add lemon juice slowly as for a mayonnaise. Fold in lemon zest by hand and season with salt and cracked black pepper. Stir butter into pasta and serve topped with pecorino cheese.

Serves 4

ohng choi on steak with fried noodles

soba noodle salad

crispy egg noodles with chicken and snowpeas

mussels with egg noodles and curry sauce

quick fish curry with noodles

red curry of beef with peanuts and spinach

chinese barbecued duck on crisp noodle cakes with spring onion and bok choy

chilli pork with vegetables and noodles

chinese roast duck with hokkien noodles

with
noodles

ohng choi on steak with fried noodles

Ohng choi has dark green spear-shaped leaves on thin stems and is also called Chinese water spinach. It is readily available at Asian food stores all year round.

4 x 150 g (5 oz) eye fillet steak

250 ml (1 cup) peanut oil for deep-frying

50 g (1½ oz) dried rice vermicelli

2 tablespoons vegetable oil

1 bunch ohng choi, *stems removed*

2 cloves garlic, finely chopped

2 teaspoons finely grated fresh ginger

2 fresh red chillies, finely sliced or to taste

*1 tablespoon oyster sauce mixed with
  1 tablespoon water*

Cook steaks on a hot barbecue or grill pan until done to your liking. Rest in a warm place.

Heat peanut oil in a large pan or wok and when hot fry vermicelli in batches until crisp and puffed. Drain on absorbent paper.

Heat vegetable oil in a large pan, add *ohng choi*, garlic, ginger and chillies and stir-fry over medium heat for 2–3 minutes, or until *ohng choi* is wilted. Add oyster sauce and stir to combine. Divide noodles between four plates. Place steak on top of noodles and top with *ohng choi*. Drizzle with the remaining pan juices.

Serves 4

| soba noodle salad

350 g (11½ oz) dried soba noodles

2 teaspoons sesame oil

2 chicken breast fillets

1 Lebanese cucumber, halved lengthways, seeded and finely sliced

1 tablespoon grated fresh ginger

6 spring onions (scallions), finely sliced

3 tablespoons mirin

4 tablespoons soya sauce

2 teaspoons lime juice

wasabi paste to taste (optional)

½ cup mint leaves, coarsely chopped

Cook noodles in boiling water for 6–8 minutes or until tender. Drain and refresh in cold water, drain again and toss in sesame oil. Cover and chill.

Pan-fry chicken breast fillets in a lightly oiled pan over medium heat until cooked. Remove and cut into thin slices.

In a large bowl combine noodles, sliced chicken, cucumber, ginger and spring onions. Mix mirin, soya sauce, lime juice and wasabi paste together and pour over noodles. Toss gently to combine. Divide salad between 4 bowls and garnish with mint leaves.

Serves 4

with noodles

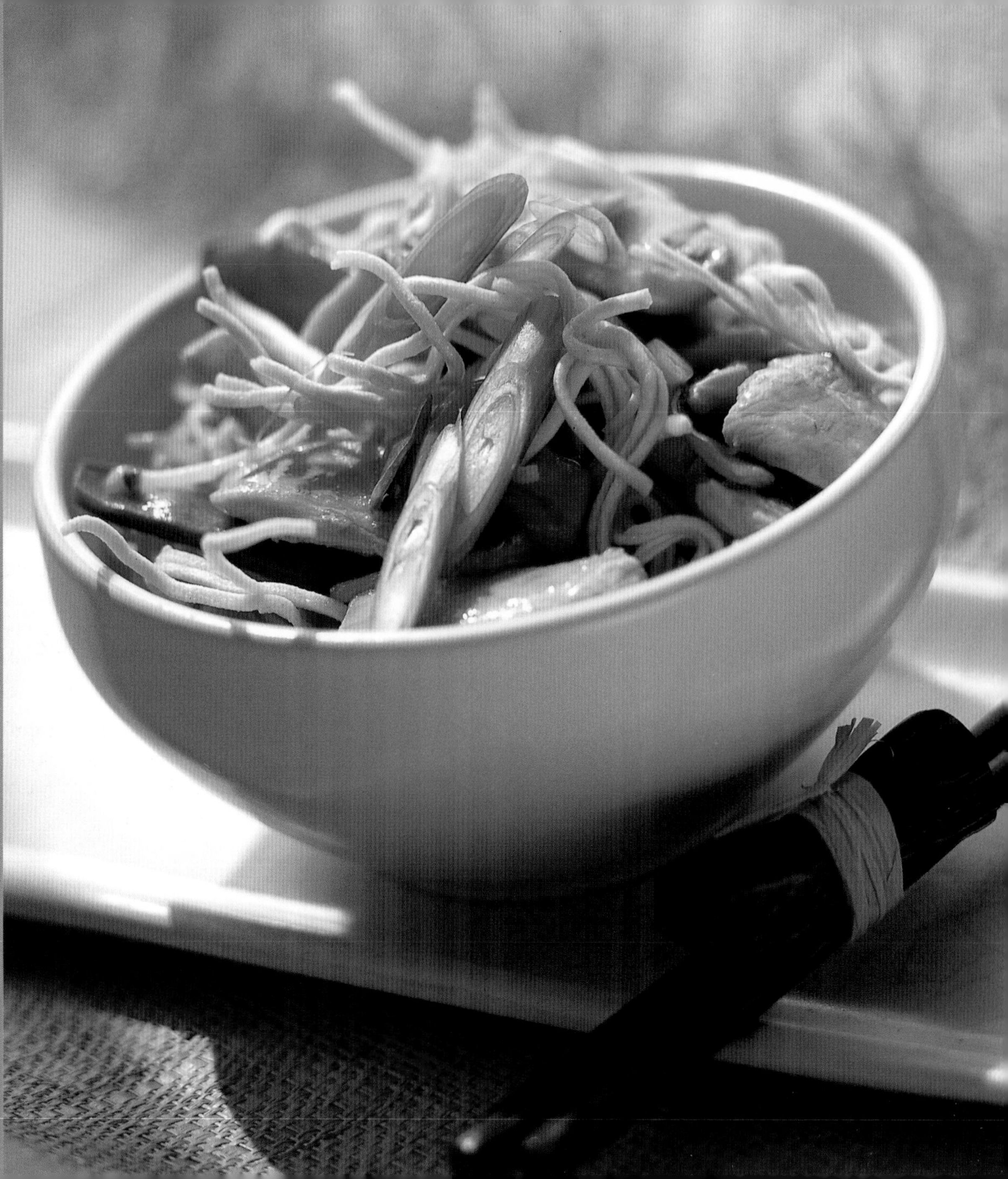

crispy egg noodles
with chicken and snowpeas

400 g (8 oz) dried egg noodles

vegetable oil for frying

3 chicken breast fillets, cut into thin strips

2 cloves garlic, finely chopped

1 tablespoon grated ginger

150 g (5 oz) snowpeas (mange-tout), trimmed

100 g (3½ oz) mushrooms, sliced

300 ml (10 fl oz) chicken stock

1 tablespoon soya sauce

2 teaspoons mirin

150 g (2 cups) beansprouts

1 tablespoon cornflour (cornstarch),
    mixed with 1 tablespoon water

4 spring onions (scallions), finely sliced

Cook noodles in plenty of salted boiling water for 3–4 minutes or until just tender. Drain and spread on absorbent paper to dry. Deep-fry noodles in hot vegetable oil in small batches until crisp. Drain well.

Pour off all but 2 tablespoons of the oil and stir-fry chicken over medium heat until just cooked. Remove and set aside.

Add 1 tablespoon of oil to wok and stir garlic and ginger over low heat until aromatic. Add snowpeas and mushrooms, and stir-fry for 1 minute. Return chicken to wok and add chicken stock, soya sauce and mirin and simmer for 1–2 minutes. Add beansprouts and stir.

Add cornflour mixture and stir until sauce thickens. Divide noodles among 4 plates and pour chicken and vegetables over noodles. Top with spring onions.

Serves 4

mussels with egg
noodles and curry sauce

A mild curry sauce complements the flavours of this delicate shellfish. Discard any mussels that do not open.

200 g (7 oz) fresh Chinese egg noodles
1 tablespoon peanut oil
2 teaspoons Thai green curry paste (see glossary)
1 clove garlic, finely chopped
500 ml (2 cups) coconut milk
2 kaffir lime leaves
1 stalk lemongrass, bruised
1 tablespoon chopped galangal or ginger
2 teaspoons fish sauce
2 teaspoons palm sugar
1 tablespoon lime juice
16 mussels, scrubbed and bearded
10 Thai basil leaves

Cook noodles in salted boiling water for 1 minute or until tender (the noodles need very little cooking – just a few quick plunge-and-lifts in boiling water will do). Drain.

Heat peanut oil in a large saucepan and cook curry paste and garlic until aromatic. Add coconut milk, lime leaves, lemongrass and galangal. Stir until boiling, reduce heat and simmer for 5 minutes, stirring from time to time. Stir in fish sauce, sugar and lime juice. Add mussels and simmer for 3–5 minutes until shells open.

Place noodles in 2 serving bowls and divide mussels between them. Discard lemongrass and lime leaves and pour sauce over. Garnish with Thai basil leaves.

Serves 2

with noodles

quick fish curry
with noodles

200 g (7 oz) dried rice vermicelli

1 tablespoon vegetable oil

3 tablespoons Thai green curry paste (see glossary)

400 ml (14 fl oz) coconut milk

140 ml (4½ fl oz) coconut cream

2 teaspoons fish sauce

500 g (1 lb) firm white fish fillets,
   cut into bite-sized pieces

1 tablespoon chopped coriander (cilantro) leaves

2 teaspoons lemon juice

15 small basil leaves, fried in olive oil until crisp
   for garnish

Cook vermicelli in boiling water for about 2 minutes or until tender. Drain.

Heat vegetable oil in a pan and add curry paste. Stir for 2–3 minutes or until aromatic. Add coconut milk, coconut cream and fish sauce and simmer over low heat for 10 minutes. Add fish pieces and chopped coriander and simmer for 3–5 minutes or until fish is just cooked. Stir in the lemon juice. Place vermicelli in 3 bowls and spoon fish curry on top. Garnish with fried basil leaves.

Serves 3

red curry of beef
with peanuts and spinach

2 tablespoons peanut oil

500 g (1 lb) lean beef, cut into thin strips

2 tablespoons Thai red curry paste (see glossary)

140 ml (4½ fl oz) coconut cream

1 tablespoon palm or brown sugar

2 tablespoons fish sauce

400 ml (14 fl oz) coconut milk

1 carrot, finely sliced

200 g (7 oz) baby corn

1 bunch spinach, stems removed

100 g (3½ oz) peanuts, lightly roasted and chopped

2 kaffir lime leaves, very finely shredded (optional)

Heat 1 tablespoon of peanut oil in wok or large pan and stir-fry beef until brown. Remove and set aside.

Add remaining tablespoon of oil and when hot add curry paste and stir for 2–3 minutes until fragrant. Add coconut cream, sugar, fish sauce and coconut milk and simmer for 5 minutes. Add carrot and corn, and cook until they are tender and crisp.

Return beef to wok, add spinach and stir until spinach is wilted. Serve sprinkled with peanuts and lime leaves. Accompany with cooked egg noodles or steamed rice.

Serves 4

chinese barbecued duck on crisp noodle cakes with spring onion and bok choy

2 spring onions (scallions)
150 g (5 oz) dried wheat noodles
1 clove garlic, finely chopped
2 spring onions (scallions), extra, finely sliced
1 tablespoon chopped mint
1 red chilli, finely sliced
peanut oil for shallow frying
leaves from 6 heads baby bok choy
1 tablespoon peanut oil
1 Chinese barbecued duck, cut into bite-sized pieces
60 ml (¼ cup) sweet chilli sauce

Cut spring onions into 6 cm (2½ in) long lengths then in half lengthways. Stand in iced water for 15 minutes or until curled. Drain.

Cook noodles in lightly salted boiling water for 3 minutes or until tender. Drain and pat dry on absorbent paper.

Combine noodles with garlic, extra spring onion, mint and red chilli and mix well.

Heat a thin layer of peanut oil in a large frying pan, add one-sixth of noodle mixture, flatten with the back of a spoon to form a disk and cook for 2–3 minutes on each side, or until crisp. Drain on absorbent paper. Repeat with the remaining mixture.

Heat 1 tablespoon of peanut oil in a wok, add bok choy and toss until wilted. Place noodle cakes on serving plates, top with bok choy, duck and spring onion curls and drizzle with sweet chilli sauce.

Serves 6

with noodles

chilli pork with
vegetables and noodles

400 g (14 oz) fresh Shanghai noodles
3 tablespoons peanut oil
450 g (15 oz) pork fillet, thinly sliced
1 clove garlic, finely chopped
1 onion, sliced
3 heads bok choy, roughly sliced
2 tomatoes, chopped
150 g (5 oz) snowpeas (mange-tout), trimmed
2 small red chillies, finely chopped or to taste
1 tablespoon palm sugar
2 tablespoons fish sauce
2 tablespoons soya sauce
60 ml (3 tablespoons) lime juice
150 g (2 cups) beansprouts
4 spring onions (scallions), finely sliced

Place noodles in a saucepan of boiling water and boil for 5 minutes. Drain and refresh in cold water.

Heat 2 tablespoons of oil in a large pan and stir-fry sliced pork fillets over medium heat until cooked. Remove.

Add remaining oil to pan and when hot add garlic, onion, bok choy and tomato and stir until onion is soft.

Add snowpeas, chillies, palm sugar, fish sauce, soya sauce and lime juice and stir.

Add noodles and thinly sliced pork with beansprouts and stir until heated through. Serve topped with sliced spring onions.

Serves 4

chinese roast duck
with hokkien noodles

500 g (1 lb) Hokkien noodles

2 tablespoons peanut oil

2 eggs, lightly beaten

½ red capsicum (bell pepper), sliced

100 g (3½ oz) mushrooms, sliced

1 Chinese roast duck, cut into bite-sized pieces

4 spring onions (scallions), sliced

2 tablespoons light soya sauce

1 tablespoon hoisin sauce

75 g (1 cup) beansprouts

*60 g (¼ cup) cashew nuts, toasted and
  roughly chopped*

Place noodles in a heatproof bowl and cover with boiling water for 30 seconds to 1 minute. Drain well.

Heat 1 tablespoon of oil in wok and add eggs. When eggs are set remove and cool.

Add remaining oil and stir-fry capsicum and mushrooms until soft. Add duck, spring onions, soya sauce and hoisin sauce and stir until heated through. Add beansprouts and stir.

Cut egg into thin strips.

Divide noodles between 4 bowls and spoon duck on top. Serve garnished with cashew nuts and sliced egg.

Serves 4

lemon myrtle fettuccine
with scallops and
oven-dried tomatoes

seafood risotto

orzo with crab,
asparagus and oven-
roasted tomatoes

crispy fried fish with
three-flavoured sauce

crab claws with
tomato sauce

scallops with sugar snap
peas and celery

spaghettini with
smoked trout

smoked salmon risotto

basque-style tuna stew

crispy fish with
bok choy and shiitake
mushrooms

from
the sea

lemon myrtle fettuccine

with scallops and oven-dried tomatoes

Full of flavour and colour, this dish is great when you're short of time. Plain fettuccine can be substituted if lemon myrtle is not available. Basil leaves are usually torn instead of chopped as cutting them with a knife discolours them.

400 g (14 oz) lemon myrtle fettuccine
2 tablespoons oil from the tomatoes (see below)
400 g (14 oz) fresh scallops
3 cloves garlic, finely chopped
125 ml (½ cup) dry white wine
90 g (½ cup) oil-packed dried tomatoes, sliced
2 teaspoons grated lime zest
juice of 1 lime
12 basil leaves, roughly torn
salt and cracked black pepper
2 tablespoons fresh oregano, chopped

Cook fettuccine in plenty of salted boiling water until *al dente*. Drain.

Sauté scallops in 1 tablespoon of oil over medium heat, stirring until just opaque. Remove and reserve scallops with liquid.

Add remaining oil to pan and sauté garlic over low heat until aromatic. Add wine and cook over high heat until reduced by half. Stir in tomatoes, lime zest, lime juice and basil and return scallops to pan.

Toss drained pasta with the scallop sauce and serve topped with cracked black pepper and oregano.

Serves 4

seafood risotto

Risotto ai frutti di mare is a magnificent dish in many regions of Italy and needs to be made with Italian rice, either Arborio, Vialone Nano or Carnaroli to achieve the creamy consistency.

It should be stirred constantly while cooking and is best made just before serving as it becomes soft and mushy on reheating.

6 tablespoons butter
1 onion, chopped
500 g (2½ cups) Arborio rice
185 ml (¾ cup) dry white wine
1.5–2 litres (6–8 cups) fish stock
100 g (3½ oz) green (raw) prawns (shrimps),
*   shelled and deveined*
100 g (3½ oz) mussels or oysters (shells removed)
100 g (3½ oz) swordfish fillet or other firm white fish,
*   cut into bite-sized pieces*
100 g (3½ oz) scallops
½ cup flat-leaf (Italian) parsley, chopped
dried chilli flakes to taste

Melt 3 tablespoons of the butter in a large pan over medium heat and add the onion. Stir until the onion is soft and pale yellow.

Add rice and stir to coat the grains well with the butter. Add wine and stir constantly until wine has evaporated. Stir in 2 ladles of fish stock or enough to just cover the rice. Continue cooking and stirring rice, adding stock, a little at a time, until the rice is half cooked.

Add seafood and mix gently. Add 1–2 ladles of stock and stir gently until rice is cooked but firm to the bite. Remove from heat and stir in the remaining butter. Pour into a serving dish and sprinkle with chopped parsley and chilli flakes.

Serves 4

orzo with crab, asparagus and oven-roasted tomatoes

I first met Glen Bowman in Bangkok where we both spent a week laughing, learning and eating at the Oriental Hotel's traditional Thai Cooking School. He has now become one of Sydney's foremost chefs with a true understanding of Australia's culinary multiculturalism.

Orzo is a rice-shaped pasta also called risoni.

4 plum (Roma) tomatoes, cut into halves

a little balsamic vinegar

dried thyme leaves

500 g (1 lb) orzo

3 stalks lemongrass, bruised

2 tablespoons butter

salt and black pepper

2 tablespoons lemon juice

1 bunch asparagus, cut into 2 cm (¾ in) pieces and blanched

1 red chilli, finely sliced (or to taste)

6 basil leaves, torn

2 tablespoons chopped coriander (cilantro) leaves

200 g (7 oz) cooked crabmeat

Sprinkle the tomato halves with a little balsamic vinegar and dried thyme leaves, then place them on a lightly greased baking tray and roast at 150°C (300°F) for 45 minutes.

Cook pasta in plenty of salted boiling water with lemongrass until *al dente*. Drain and discard lemongrass.

Cut butter into pieces and stir through pasta. Add salt and pepper to taste. Add lemon juice and stir. Add asparagus, chilli, basil and coriander, and stir. Add crabmeat and toss gently to combine. Serve topped with roasted tomatoes.

Serves 4

crispy fried fish with
three-flavoured sauce

The sauce for this recipe by chef Paul Blain can be made ahead and reheated, leaving only the fish to be cooked at the last minute. This dish is 'three-flavoured' because the sauce is at once sweet, sour and hot.

Tamarind pulp is available in blocks from Asian food stores.

1.2 kg (2 lb 7 oz) whole red reef fish,
  cleaned and scaled
1 tablespoon sea salt

Tamarind Water
75 g (3 tablespoons) tamarind pulp
250 ml (1 cup) boiling water

Sauce
4 cloves garlic
2 coriander (cilantro) roots
6 large red chillies, split, seeded and coarsely chopped
vegetable oil for deep-frying
6 kaffir lime leaves, very finely sliced
4 tablespoons palm sugar
1 tablespoon Thai fish sauce
deep-fried basil leaves for garnish

Score both sides of the fish in a diamond pattern and rub with sea salt. Open the centre so it stands upright, fixing the position with satay sticks. Leave in this position while preparing the sauce.

To make tamarind water, soak tamarind pulp in boiling water for 10 minutes. Strain before use.

To make the sauce, pound the garlic and coriander to a paste in a mortar and pestle (or use a blender). Add the chillies and pound or process. Fry the paste in 2 tablespoons of oil until slightly roasted. Add lime leaves and palm sugar. Continue frying and stirring until the mixture lightly caramelises. Season with fish sauce. Add tamarind water and reduce slightly to a thickened syrup.

Heat a large pan filled to a depth of 10–12 cm (4–5 in) with oil. Fry the fish until the skin crisps and the flesh flakes away from the bone easily, 8–10 minutes, depending on the thickness. Remove from the oil using an egglift and a pair of tongs, and stand upright on a serving plate. Pour the sauce over the fish. Garnish with deep-fried basil leaves and serve with steamed jasmine rice.

Serves 2

crab claws with
tomato sauce

1.5 kg (3 lb) green (raw) crabs
500 ml (2 cups) water
1 teaspoon salt
1 teaspoon peppercorns
2 sprigs thyme
2 sprigs flat-leaf (Italian) parsley
1 bay leaf
1 tablespoon olive oil
1 onion, roughly chopped
1 clove garlic, finely chopped
1 x 400 g (14 oz) can tomatoes, undrained
sugar, salt and cayenne pepper to taste
4 slices from a french breadstick
extra olive oil
1 extra whole garlic clove
extra flat-leaf (Italian) parsley for garnish

Remove top shell from crabs and cut each crab into serving portions. Remove the bottom shell, leaving the legs intact.

Place water, salt, peppercorns, thyme, parsley and bay leaf in a large saucepan and bring to the boil. Poach crab pieces for 2–4 minutes or until the shells change colour. Drain and reserve ½ cup of the poaching liquid.

Heat olive oil in a saucepan and cook onion and garlic over medium heat until soft. Add tomatoes and juices, sugar, salt and cayenne to taste, and simmer for 20 minutes. Blend in a food processor until almost smooth. Stir in the reserved poaching liquid.

Brush both sides of the bread with olive oil and rub with a bruised clove of garlic. Grill bread until golden.

Divide tomato sauce between 2 deep bowls, top each with 2 slices of toast and portions of crab. Garnish with parsley and serve warm or at room temperature.

Provide crab crackers and finger bowls.

Serves 2

scallops with sugar snap peas and celery

2 tablespoons vegetable oil
125 g (4 oz) sugar snap peas, strings removed
2 sticks celery, sliced
1 small carrot, julienned
5 spring onions (scallions), sliced
1 clove garlic, finely chopped
2 teaspoons finely grated fresh ginger
2 teaspoons cornflour (cornstarch)
1 tablespoon soya sauce
125 ml (1/2 cup) water
50 g (1 1/2 oz) baby spinach leaves
250 g (8 oz) scallops
1/2 teaspoon sesame oil

Heat vegetable oil in a wok and stir-fry peas, celery and carrot for 1 minute. Add spring onions, garlic and ginger and stir-fry for 30 seconds. Remove from wok.

Mix cornflour with soya sauce and water, pour into wok and stir until thickened. Add spinach and scallops and simmer for 1 minute, until scallops just turn opaque and spinach is wilted. Return vegetables to wok and add sesame oil. Stir to combine and serve with cooked thin egg noodles or steamed rice.

Serves 2–3

spaghettini with smoked trout

400 g (14 oz) spaghettini
2 tablespoons butter
2 brown shallots, chopped
200 g (7 oz) smoked trout, cut into strips
200 ml (7 fl oz) pouring cream
cracked black pepper
2 spring onions (scallions), finely sliced
1 tablespoon chopped fresh dill

Cook pasta in plenty of salted boiling water until *al dente*. Drain.

Melt butter in a pan over medium heat and add shallots. Stir until soft, add half the smoked trout, cream and stir until heated through. Remove and blend in a food processor until smooth.

Add the sauce to pasta and stir to combine. Add remaining trout pieces and black pepper and stir gently. Serve topped with spring onions and dill.

Serves 4

smoked salmon
risotto

Gabriele Ferron operates the Riseria Ferron (Ferron Rice Mill) just a few kilometres from Verona in northern Italy which has been run by his father and his grandfather before him. The rice mill has been in operation since the 1650s and is water-powered by the original seven-metre wheel and pure underground spring water surfacing in canals throughout the valley of Verona. The rice is grown without any pesticide and retains flavour and nutritional qualities often lost in modern mass production.

Ferron rice is perfect for risotto; the larger, longer-grained Carnaroli is slightly less absorbent than Vialone Nano and so remains slightly more *al dente*; both are delicious in the following recipe. Ferron cooks the rice by the absorption method, which is in contrast to the traditional gradual addition of stock.

2 tablespoons extra-virgin olive oil
1 onion, finely chopped
400 g (14 oz) Italian rice (Arborio, Carnaroli or Vialone Nano)
800 ml (3¼ cups) vegetable stock, boiling
60 g (¼ cup) butter
1 sprig rosemary
150 g (5 oz) smoked salmon, cut into bite-sized pieces
black pepper
1 tablespoon butter, extra

Heat olive oil in a large saucepan and add onion. Stir over medium heat until soft. Add rice and mix well. Stir until rice is well coated with oil. Add boiling stock, stir gently, cover and cook over very low heat for about 18 minutes or until rice is *al dente*.

Heat butter in a small pan and when foaming add rosemary. Stir until wilted and add smoked salmon and black pepper. Remove from heat, discard rosemary.

When rice is cooked remove from heat and stir in 1 tablespoon butter and gently fold in the salmon. Serve immediately.

Serves 3–4

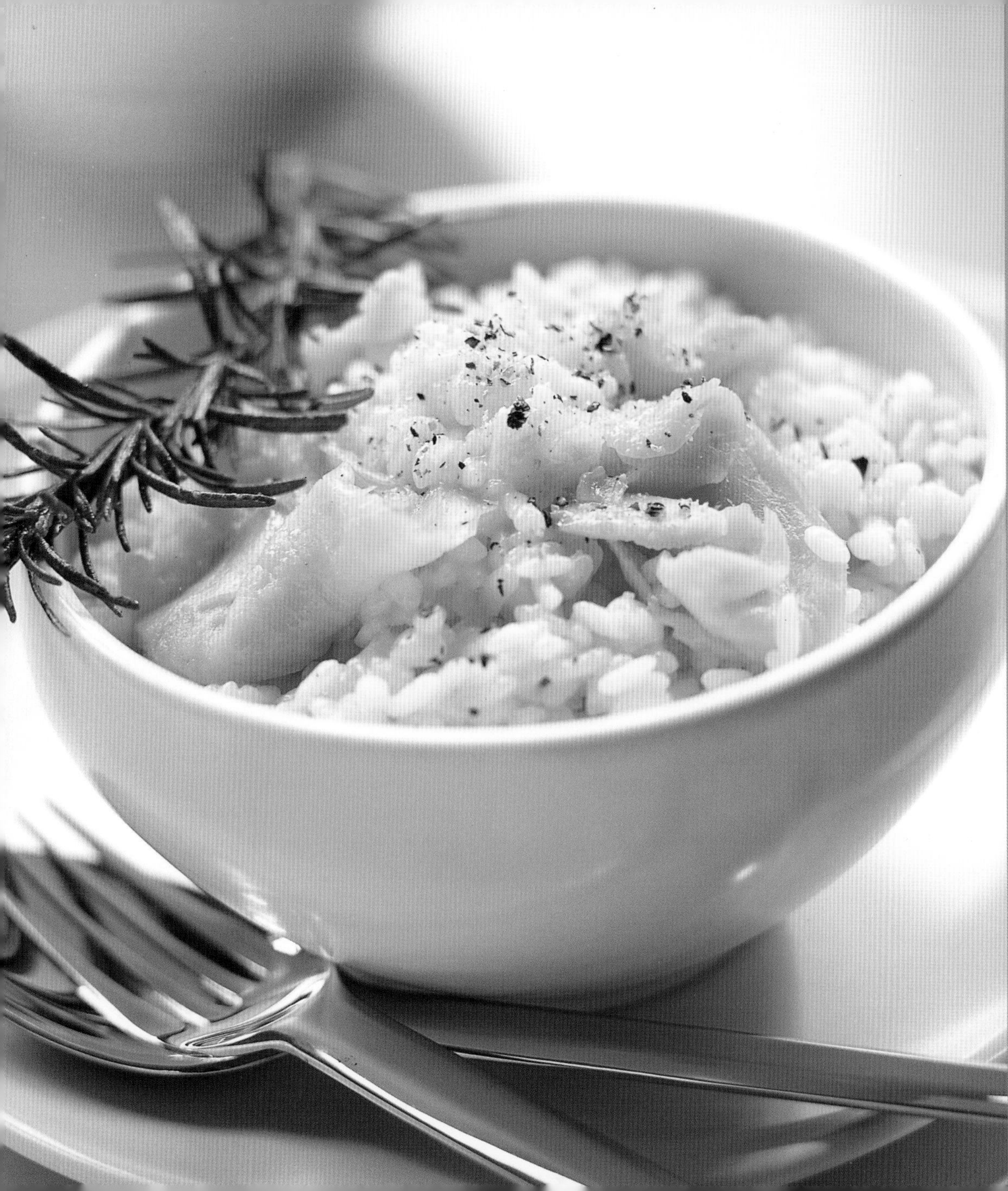

from the sea

basque-style
tuna stew

San Sebastian-Donostia is a small city nestled at the foot of Mount Urgull in northern Spain just 16 km (10 miles) from the French border. Students travel from all over the world to learn the secrets of the New Basque Cuisine in this picturesque bustling fishing port where Luis Irizar is known as the 'Father of Basque Gastronomy'.

A trip down narrow cobblestoned streets early one morning with Irizar brought joyous shouts of recognition from tapas bar and restaurant owners as they greeted him on the way to the local markets. Once inside the markets, vendors appeared from behind their stalls with enthusiastic backslapping and hand shaking. It was very evident that Irizar was highly regarded as one of Spain's gastronomic leaders. In San Sebastian I enjoyed this dish with bonito but it is equally delicious with tuna or salmon and lots of good crusty bread to mop up the sauce.

100 ml (3½ oz) extra-virgin olive oil
2 onions, chopped
1 red capsicum (bell pepper), sliced
1 green capsicum (bell pepper), sliced
4 plum (Roma) tomatoes, chopped
2 pieces sun-dried capsicum (bell pepper)
4 potatoes, peeled and cut into 2 cm (¾ in) pieces
1 litre (4 cups) fish stock
125 ml (½ cup) dry white wine
750 g (1½ lb) fresh tuna, cut into 3 cm (1½ in) pieces
3 tablespoons chopped flat-leaf (Italian) parsley
salt and pepper

Heat oil in a large, heavy-based saucepan and cook onion and capsicums over medium heat until onion is soft. Add tomatoes, sun-dried capsicum, potato, stock and wine and simmer, uncovered, over medium heat for about 20 minutes or until potato is cooked.

Add tuna pieces and cook for 2–3 minutes. Remove from the heat and stir in parsley, salt and pepper and cover and stand for 5 minutes before serving with crusty bread.

Serves 6

crispy fish with
bok choy and shiitake mushrooms

6 dried shiitake mushrooms

750 g (1½ lb) fish fillets, cut into bite-sized pieces

60 g (½ cup) cornflour (cornstarch)

vegetable oil for deep-frying

1 tablespoon safflower oil

leaves from 3 heads bok choy

4 spring onions (scallions), sliced

1 clove garlic, finely chopped

1 teaspoon finely grated fresh ginger

2 fresh red chillies, finely chopped or to taste

2 tablespoons soya sauce

a pinch of five-spice powder

1 teaspoon caster (superfine) sugar

3 teaspoons cornflour (cornstarch),
    mixed with 2 tablespoons water

Soak mushrooms in hot water for 20 minutes. Drain, reserving the soaking water, discard stems and slice.

Toss fish pieces in cornflour and shake off excess. Heat vegetable oil in large pan or wok and when very hot add half the fish and deep-fry for about 2 minutes or until cooked. Drain on absorbent paper. Repeat with remaining fish.

Discard oil and add safflower oil to wok. Heat and add bok choy. Stir until wilted. Add sliced mushrooms, spring onions, garlic, ginger, chillies and stir. Add soya sauce, five-spice powder, sugar and ¾ cup of the strained mushroom liquid and simmer for 3 minutes. Add cornflour mixture and bring to the boil, stirring until sauce thickens. Pour over fish and serve with crisp-fried rice noodles or steamed rice.

Serves 4

gado gado

sweet and sour
eggplant salad

beef noodle salad

spicy chicken with rice
noodles and herb salad

asian prawn and
cucumber salad

cotechino with white
beans and greens in
thyme vinaigrette

cavatappi, prosciutto
and goat's cheese salad

steamed salmon with
glass noodles

pomelo and prawn salad

tuna, quail egg and
bean salad

pork and green mango
salad

salads

gado gado

One of the most versatile Indonesian vegetable dishes, this recipe makes a delicious light lunch or can be served on top of cooked egg noodles. The peanut sauce is great served with grilled lamb chops.

Snake beans are known by various names including asparagus beans, Chinese long beans and yard beans. These narrow beans are dark green and stringless. They taste similar to a green bean, but have a denser texture.

vegetable oil for frying

250 g (8 oz) firm tofu, cut into 2 cm (¾ in) pieces

1 carrot, cut into thin strips and blanched

½ bunch snake beans (about 100 g [3½ oz]), cut into short lengths and blanched

3 hard-boiled eggs, quartered

150 g (2 cups) beansprouts

100 g (1 cup) shredded cabbage, blanched

1 red capsicum (bell pepper), cut into strips

lettuce leaves

Peanut Sauce

1 tablespoon vegetable oil

1 clove garlic, finely chopped

2 teaspoons freshly grated ginger

4 shallots, finely chopped

2–3 fresh red chillies, finely chopped

1 tablespoon palm sugar

185 ml (¾ cup) water

a pinch of salt

8 tablespoons peanut butter

185 ml (¾ cup) coconut milk

1 tablespoon kecap manis (see glossary)

1 tablespoon lemon juice

Heat oil in a wok or pan and fry tofu until crisp and golden. Drain on absorbent paper.

To make the peanut sauce, heat vegetable oil in wok and stir-fry garlic, ginger and shallots until aromatic. Add chillies, palm sugar, water, salt and peanut butter and stir-fry for 2 minutes.
Add coconut milk, kecap manis and lemon juice and stir over low heat until the sauce thickens.

Arrange tofu, vegetables and eggs on a platter lined with the lettuce leaves and serve with peanut sauce.

Serves 4

sweet and sour
eggplant salad

Caponata is popular all over Sicily, and this version by Carla Tomasi is one of the best I've tasted. She suggests serving it cool with a slice of very fresh ricotta cheese. It can also be expanded to make a substantial meal: fold 250 g (8 oz) cooked penne through it after the vegetables are cooked.

600 g (1¼ lb) eggplant (aubergine)
salt
peanut oil for frying
125 ml (½ cup) extra-virgin olive oil
2 sticks celery, finely sliced
1 medium onion, finely sliced
500 g (1 lb) ripe tomatoes, chopped
1 tablespoon salted capers, rinsed
1 tablespoon sultanas
75 g (about ½ cup) green olives
1 tablespoon pinenuts
1 tablespoon red-wine vinegar
1 tablespoon caster (superfine) sugar
salt and black pepper

Cut eggplant into large cubes, sprinkle with salt and rest for 20–30 minutes. Rinse eggplant and pat dry with absorbent paper. Fry in hot peanut oil until cooked and golden. Drain on absorbent paper and set aside.

Heat olive oil in a large frying pan and add celery and onion and cook until soft. Add tomatoes and cook, stirring occasionally, for about 5 minutes or until thick. Add remaining ingredients and stir well. Adjust seasoning and simmer for 15 minutes. Add eggplant and stir to combine. Set aside to cool.

Serves 4

beef noodle salad

A tasty but slightly simplified variation on the renowned Thai beef salad.

200 g (7 oz) dried wheat noodles

1 tablespoon vegetable oil

6 shallots, very finely sliced

500 g (1 lb) rump or fillet steak, grilled medium-rare
and sliced thinly

200 g (7 oz) snowpeas (mange-tout), trimmed
and blanched

150 g (5 oz/2 cups) beansprouts

100 g (3½ oz) snowpea (mange-tout) shoots

1 red capsicum (bell pepper), finely sliced

3 small red chillies or to taste

1 Lebanese cucumber, peeled and cut into
6 cm x 1 cm (2½ in x ½ in) pieces

½ cup coriander (cilantro) leaves

½ cup mint leaves

2 tablespoons sesame seeds, toasted

Dressing

4 tablespoons extra-virgin olive oil

2 tablespoons soya sauce

1 teaspoon fish sauce

2 tablespoons white-wine vinegar

1 clove garlic, finely chopped

2 teaspoons freshly grated ginger

Cook dried noodles in boiling water for 3–5 minutes or until soft and separated. Drain.

Heat vegetable oil and fry shallots until golden and crisp. Drain on absorbent paper.

In a large bowl combine sliced beef, snowpeas, beansprouts, snowpea shoots, capsicum, chillies, cucumber, coriander and mint leaves. Toss gently to combine.

To make the dressing, place all ingredients in a small bowl and whisk until well combined.

Add noodles to vegetables. Pour over the dressing, toss gently and divide evenly between 6 bowls.

Top with fried shallots and sprinkle with sesame seeds before serving.

Serves 6

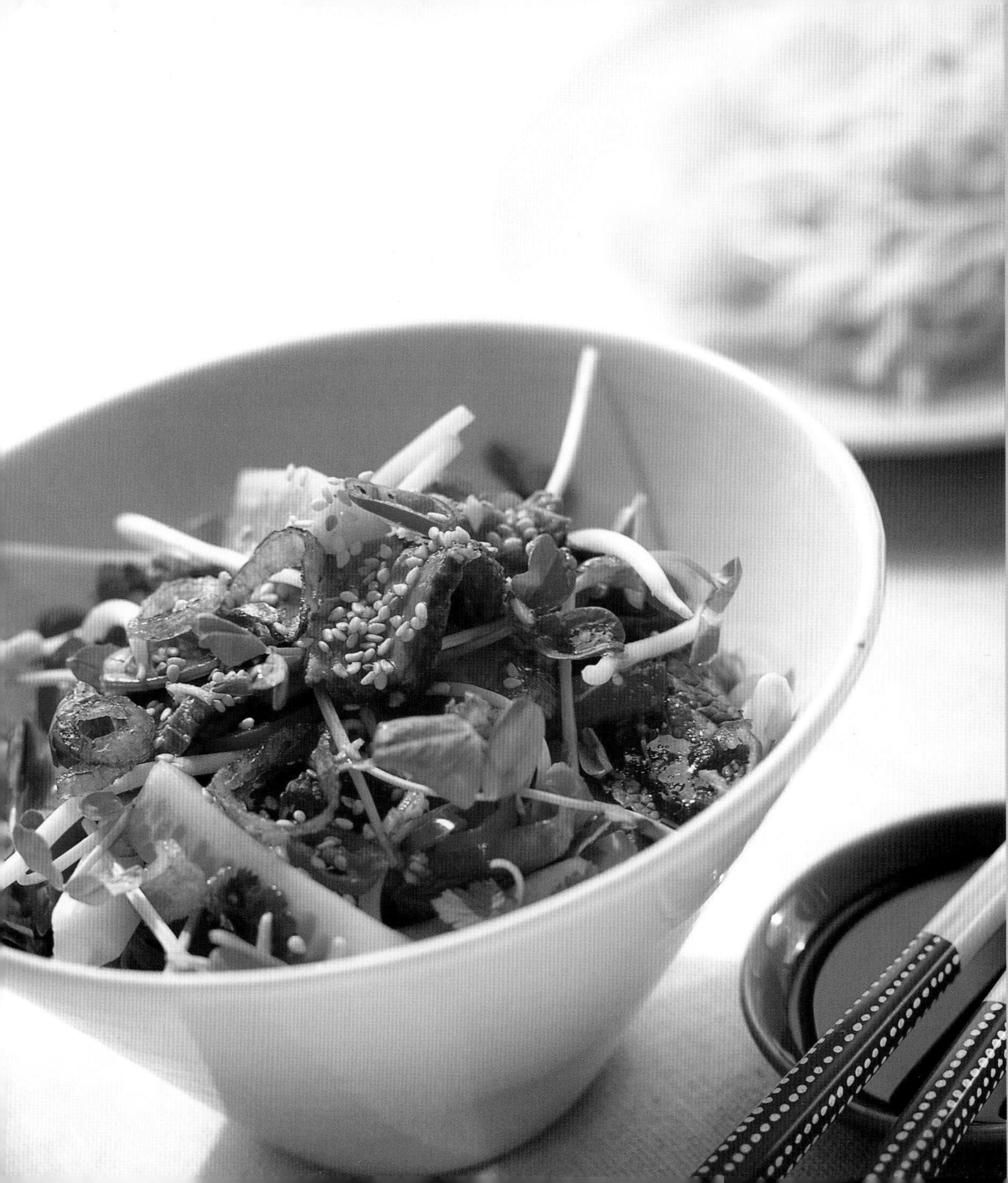

salads

spicy chicken
with rice noodles and herb salad

This herb salad recipe is the creation of Australian chef, Paul Blain.

Chilli paste in soya bean oil (*nam prik pao*) is available at Asian food stores.

500 g (1 lb) fresh wide rice noodles

2 tablespoons vegetable oil

800 g (1¾ lb) chicken thigh fillets, cut into thin strips

3 tablespoons chilli paste in soya bean oil (chilli jam), or to taste

2 tablespoons fish sauce

250 ml (1 cup) coconut cream

½ cup garlic chives, cut into 2 cm (¾ in) lengths

½ cup coriander (cilantro) leaves

3 spring onions (scallions), finely sliced

1 cup basil leaves

Cut the rice noodles into 2 cm (¾ in) lengths and microwave on high for 1 minute. Separate the layers and set aside.

Heat vegetable oil in a wok and when hot add the chicken and stir-fry for 4–5 minutes. Add the chilli paste and stir to coat the chicken. Add fish sauce and stir. Turn heat to medium and add coconut cream. When cream comes to a simmer add the rice noodles and stir to heat through. Add chives, coriander leaves, spring onions and basil leaves and stir. Remove from heat and serve.

Serves 4

asian prawn and
cucumber salad

*600 g (1¼ lb) cooked medium-sized prawns (shrimps),
  shelled and deveined*

1 red capsicum (bell pepper), finely sliced

1 small red onion, sliced

*2 Lebanese cucumbers, halved lengthways,
  seeded and sliced*

3 teaspoons fish sauce

2 teaspoons palm or brown sugar

3 tablespoons lemon juice

1 stick lemongrass, white portion only, very finely sliced

1 fresh red chilli or to taste

salad leaves or lettuce leaves

½ cup fresh mint leaves

Place prawns, capsicum, onion and cucumbers in a large bowl.

Combine fish sauce, palm sugar, lemon juice, lemongrass and chilli in a small bowl and stir until sugar is dissolved. Pour dressing over prawns and toss gently to combine.

Serve on a bed of crisp salad leaves and garnish with mint leaves.

Serves 4

cotechino with white beans and greens in thyme vinaigrette

Cotechino is a large lightly cured Italian pork sausage which is always cooked before serving. Usually poached or steamed, it is eaten hot, often with mashed potatoes. The cannellini beans could be replaced with cooked pasta for an appetising variation.

1 cotechino sausage

200 g (7 oz) dried cannellini beans, soaked in cold water overnight and drained

bouquet garni (see glossary)

1 small onion, peeled and cut in half

185 ml (¾ cup) extra-virgin olive oil

60 ml (¼ cup) red-wine vinegar

½ teaspoon Dijon mustard

2 teaspoons fresh thyme leaves

salt and black pepper

100 g (3½ oz) mixed salad leaves

Cook cotechino in simmering water for 1¼–1½ hours. Drain and cut into thick slices.

Place beans, bouquet garni and onion in a medium saucepan and cover with cold water. Bring to the boil and simmer for 30 minutes or until beans are tender. Drain beans and discard bouquet garni and onion.

Whisk olive oil, vinegar, mustard, thyme, salt and pepper together and pour half the mixture over the hot beans. Stir to combine.

Toss the remaining vinaigrette with the salad leaves. Divide the leaves among 4 plates. Top with the cannellini beans and cotechino. Garnish with extra thyme if desired.

Serves 4

cavatappi, prosciutto and goat's cheese salad

Cavatappi is a corkscrew-shaped pasta.

250 g (8 oz) cavatappi
3 large ripe tomatoes, peeled and chopped
120 g (¾ cup) Ligurian olives
200 g (7 oz) (about 12 thin slices) prosciutto,
*   cut into strips*
2 tablespoons balsamic vinegar
185 ml (¾ cup) extra-virgin olive oil
salt and freshly ground pepper
150 g (5 oz) goat's cheese, cut into small pieces
½ cup flat-leaf (Italian) parsley leaves
¼ cup fresh basil leaves, torn

Cook pasta in plenty of salted boiling water until *al dente*. Drain. Rinse in cold water and drain again. Place in a large serving dish. Add tomatoes, olives and proscuitto and toss to combine.

In a small bowl whisk vinegar, olive oil and salt and pepper. Pour half the mixture over the pasta. Add the cheese, parsley and basil and toss to combine. Serve the salad immediately and pass around any remaining dressing.

Serves 4

steamed salmon
with glass noodles

This is another excellent recipe from one of Australia's most innovative Thai chefs, Paul Blain.

Glass noodles are known by several names including bean thread noodles and cellophane noodles. Red Chinese vinegar is available at Asian food stores; rice vinegar could, however, be substituted.

100 g (3½ oz) bean thread noodles

30 ml (1½ tablespoons) soya sauce

20 ml (1 tablespoon) red Chinese vinegar

10 ml (2 teaspoons) fish sauce

5 ml (1 teaspoon) sesame oil

1 clove garlic, finely chopped

6 choy sum leaves with stems, coarsely chopped

6 oyster mushrooms

300 g (10 oz) salmon fillet, skinned and cut into 4 pieces

10 ml (2 teaspoons) lime juice

3 spring onions (scallions), finely sliced

½ cup coriander (cilantro) leaves

Soak noodles in hot water for 10 minutes. Drain well.

Combine soya sauce, vinegar, fish sauce, sesame oil and garlic in a small bowl. Pour sauce mixture over noodles and toss gently. Place noodles on a plate or flat bowl that will fit inside a steamer, reserving the juices. Place choy sum and oyster mushrooms on top of noodles. Place salmon on top of vegetables. Add lime juice to reserved juices, stir and pour over the salmon.

Bring steamer to a simmer and place plate or bowl inside. Steam for 3–5 minutes or until done to your liking. Remove and serve garnished with spring onions and coriander leaves.

Serves 2

pomelo and
prawn salad

Pomelos look like large grapefruit, and have thick rough skins, pink flesh and a mildly acidic flavour. Oranges or grapefruit can be substituted in this recipe if pomelos are not in season.

2 tablespoons vegetable oil

2 shallots, finely sliced

1 clove garlic, finely sliced

½ large pomelo, segmented and all pith removed

300 g (10 oz) cooked prawns (shrimps), peeled and deveined, tails intact

1 tablespoon peanuts, roasted and roughly chopped

2 fresh green chillies, finely sliced (or to taste)

2 teaspoons fish sauce

2 teaspoons palm or brown sugar

juice of ½ lime

2 tablespoons coconut cream

¼ cup coriander (cilantro) leaves

2 tablespoons flaked coconut, toasted

Heat oil in a small pan and add shallots and garlic. Stir-fry 2–3 minutes or until fragrant. Drain.

Flake the flesh from the segmented pomelo. Place the shallot mixture and pomelo in a large bowl. Add prawns, peanuts and chilli.

Whisk fish sauce, palm sugar, lime juice and coconut cream in a small bowl until sugar is dissolved. Pour over pomelo mixture and toss gently to combine. Serve salad garnished with coriander leaves and toasted coconut.

Serves 2

salads

tuna, quail egg
and bean salad

500 g (1 lb) fresh borlotti beans (unshelled)

1 x 185 g can tuna in oil

12 quail eggs, hard-boiled and shelled

*100 g (3½ oz) whole baby green beans,
  blanched and refreshed under cold water*

80 g (½ cup) small black Ligurian olives

250 g (8 oz) cherry tomatoes, halved

1 capsicum (bell pepper), roasted, peeled and sliced

2 tablespoons lemon juice

2 tablespoons extra-virgin olive oil

salt and cracked black pepper

Shell borlotti beans and cook in boiling water for 25–30 minutes or until tender. Drain.

Drain tuna, reserving the oil, and place meat in a large bowl. Add eggs, green beans, olives, tomatoes, capsicum and cooked borlotti beans. Whisk 2 tablespoons of oil from tuna with lemon juice, olive oil, salt and black pepper. Pour dressing over salad and toss gently to combine.

Serve with crusty Italian bread.

Serves 4

pork and green mango salad

50 g (1½ oz) dried rice vermicelli

250 ml (1 cup) peanut oil

200 g (7 oz) snake beans, cut into 6 cm
(2½ in) lengths

400 g (14 oz) cooked pork, sliced thinly

1 green mango, peeled and finely sliced

75 g (1 cup) beansprouts

2 tablespoons unsalted roasted peanuts, crushed

¼ cup coriander (cilantro) leaves

Dressing

2 small red chillies, finely sliced

2 cloves garlic, finely chopped

1 brown shallot, very finely chopped

2 tablespoons fish sauce

3 tablespoons lime juice

2 teaspoons palm sugar

1 tablespoon sweet chilli sauce

2 teaspoons soya sauce

Shallow-fry vermicelli in hot peanut oil until crisp and puffed. Remove and drain on absorbent paper.

Blanch beans in lightly salted boiling water for 1 minute. Drain and refresh under cold water.

Combine pork with beans, mango, beansprouts and peanuts in a large bowl.

Mix all the dressing ingredients in a small bowl until sugar is dissolved. Add dressing to pork mixture and toss gently to combine.

To assemble, divide vermicelli between 4 serving plates. Place pork salad on vermicelli and top with coriander leaves.

Serves 4

the
soup
pot

thai chicken and
coconut soup

The Bangkok Oriental Hotel has a colonial-style elegance in a very exotic eastern setting. Chalie Amatyakul was the Director of the Thai Cooking School for many years and it was with him I first tasted this soup (*Gai Tom Kha*) – his tasty version had many more chillies!

The addition of fresh rice noodles makes it an interesting variation.

750 ml (3 cups) coconut milk
1.25 litres (5 cups) chicken stock
2 shallots, very finely sliced
2 small fresh red chillies, finely chopped or to taste
1 tablespoon finely grated galangal
2 x 240 g (8 oz) chicken breast fillets,
  cut into bite-sized pieces
2 tablespoons fish sauce
2 tablespoons lime juice
1 teaspoon palm sugar
300 g (10 oz) fresh rice noodles
2 kaffir lime leaves, very finely shredded
1/2 cup coriander (cilantro) leaves

Combine coconut milk, chicken stock, shallots, chillies and galangal in a large saucepan and simmer over low heat for 10 minutes.

Add chicken pieces and simmer for 5–10 minutes or until chicken is cooked. Add fish sauce, lime juice and sugar, and stir.

Place noodles in a heatproof bowl and cover with boiling water. Separate noodles, then drain. Divide noodles among 4 deep soup bowls. Ladle soup over noodles and garnish with lime leaves and coriander.

Serves 4

vietnamese beef soup with fresh rice noodles

Pho bo is often referred to as Vietnam's national dish and is eaten at any time of the day. Separate aromatic seasonings such as chillies, hoisin sauce and Vietnamese mint are often served on the side. *Pho gai* is made with chicken instead of beef and is just as delicious.

1 tablespoon vegetable oil

1 clove garlic, finely chopped

1 small brown onion, chopped

4 cm (1½ in) piece fresh ginger, finely sliced

1 litre (2 pints) water

1.5 litres (6 cups) beef stock

1 stick cinnamon

1 star anise

1 stick lemongrass

1 tablespoon fish sauce

1 tablespoon soya sauce

1 teaspoon caster (superfine) sugar

500 g (14 oz) fresh rice noodles

200 g (7 oz) eye fillet beef, very thinly sliced

2 tablespoons coriander (cilantro) leaves, roughly chopped

110 g (1½ cups) beansprouts

½ lime, cut into 4 wedges

4 spring onions (scallions), thinly sliced

3 small fresh red chillies, very finely sliced or to taste

Heat oil in a large pan and add garlic, onion and ginger and stir-fry until aromatic. Add water, stock, cinnamon, star anise, lemongrass, fish sauce, soya sauce, and sugar and bring to the boil. Simmer stock, uncovered, for 30 minutes. Strain stock, return to the saucepan and bring back to the boil.

Place rice noodles in a bowl and cover with boiling water, separate and drain. Divide noodles between 4 deep bowls. Top with beef, coriander, beansprouts and lime wedges and pour over the boiling stock. Garnish with spring onions and chillies.

Serves 4

prawn laksa

Many variations of this spicy soup can be found throughout Asia.

Prawn stock can be made by simmering the heads and shells from the prawns, or use fish stock.

200 g (7 oz) rice vermicelli

2 cloves garlic

1½ teaspoons turmeric powder

2 teaspoons ground coriander (cilantro)

2 sticks lemongrass, chopped

4 spring onions (scallions), sliced

2 teaspoons dried shrimp paste (available at Asian food stores)

1 tablespoon chopped fresh ginger

2–3 fresh red chillies or to taste

1 tablespoon peanut oil

2.25 litres (9 cups) prawn or chicken stock

1 tablespoon palm sugar

2 tablespoons fish sauce

750 ml (3 cups) coconut milk

1 kg (2 lb) medium-sized green (raw) prawns (shrimps), shelled and deveined, tails intact

150 g (2 cups) beansprouts

½ cup Vietnamese (laksa) mint leaves

½ cup coriander (cilantro) leaves

Add vermicelli to large pan of boiling water and cook for 5–6 minutes or until just tender. Drain.

Combine garlic, turmeric, coriander, lemongrass, spring onions, shrimp paste, ginger and chillies in a blender and process to a paste.

Heat oil in a wok over low heat and add the paste. Stir for a few minutes until aromatic. Add stock and simmer for 10 minutes.

Add palm sugar, fish sauce, coconut milk and prawns, stir and cook over low heat until prawns just change colour.

Divide noodles among 6 bowls. Pour sauce and prawns over noodles. Top with beansprouts, mint leaves and coriander leaves.

Serves 6

kabocha, bean
and orzo soup

Kabocha is a squash-like pumpkin grown in large quantities in Tasmania and exported to Japan, where it is considered a great delicacy. Regular pumpkin can be substituted in this recipe.

Orzo is a soup pasta the shape of elongated rice grains but if it is not available use stellette (a star-shaped pasta) or spaghettini broken into 2 cm (¾ in) lengths.

150 g (5 oz) dried kidney beans, soaked in cold water overnight and drained

500 g (1 lb) peeled and seeded kabocha or pumpkin, cut into bite-sized pieces

1 clove garlic, finely chopped

2 tablespoons extra-virgin olive oil

1 litre (2 pints) chicken stock

1 tablespoon tomato paste

150 g (5 oz) orzo or other soup pasta

1 bunch English spinach, stems removed

salt and cracked black pepper

2–3 sprigs thyme

shaved parmesan

Cook beans in unsalted water until tender. Drain and set aside.

In a large saucepan stir kabocha and garlic with olive oil over medium heat until well coated. Add chicken stock, tomato paste and orzo and cook over low heat for 8–10 minutes or until pasta is *al dente*.

Add beans and spinach leaves and season with salt and black pepper. Stir and cook over low heat until spinach is wilted. Ladle soup into bowls and garnish with thyme leaves and shaved parmesan.

Serves 4

vegetable broth
with shimeji mushrooms

Shimeji mushrooms are originally from Japan and grow in clusters. They have a mild flavour similar to oyster mushrooms and range in colour from tawny white to woody brown depending on growing conditions.

80 g (2½ oz) drained and sliced bamboo shoots
1 small carrot, julienned
180 g (6 oz) lotus root, sliced
40 g (1 oz) gingko nuts (canned)
4 spring onions (scallions), sliced
1 litre (2 pints) chicken stock
1 tablespoon soya sauce
2 teaspoons grated fresh ginger
80 g (2½ oz) shimeji *mushrooms*

Divide bamboo shoots, carrot, lotus root, gingko nuts and spring onions between 4 deep soup bowls.

Pour over near-boiling chicken stock and add a teaspoon of soya sauce to each bowl. Add ½ teaspoon of grated ginger to each bowl and stir. Top with *shimeji* mushrooms and serve immediately.

Serves 4

cannellini and
prawn soup

Wedged between the Alps and the sea, Liguria is one of Italy's most picturesque areas. It also produces distinct regional food made from tasty fish caught in the gulf of Genoa, vegetables grown in abundance on the hillsides and pungent basil that spills out of numerous glasshouses.

Angelo Parracucchi is the chef and owner of the famous Locanda dell'Angelo in the Magra River valley and his delicious bean and scampi soup is made with fresh white toscanelli beans from Tuscany. My variation, made with dried cannellini beans, is a good starter for a winter dinner party.

1.25 litres (2½ pints) chicken stock
350 g (1¾ cups) dried cannellini beans, soaked in cold water for 6 hours or overnight
2 sticks celery, chopped
1 onion, chopped
1 small carrot, chopped
2 sprigs thyme
2 sprigs flat-leaf (Italian) parsley
1 clove garlic, chopped
salt and cracked black pepper
12–18 cooked prawns (shrimps), peeled and deveined, tails intact
60 ml (¼ cup) extra-virgin olive oil

Bring chicken stock to the boil in a large saucepan and add drained beans, celery, onion, carrot, herbs and garlic. Cover and simmer over low heat for 30–45 minutes or until beans are tender. Drain beans and vegetables, reserving the stock. Discard herbs.

Process beans and vegetables in a food processor, in batches, with 3–4 cups of stock, until the desired consistency is reached. Return soup to the pan, season to taste and heat through. Serve in warm soup bowls, topped with prawns, drizzled with olive oil and sprinkled with cracked black pepper.

Serves 6

chickpea and
vegetable soup

Chickpeas are also called garbanzo beans and their cooking time can take from 30–45 minutes. They are usually sold dried but are also available canned. If using the dried, cook in unsalted water or they will toughen.

2 tablespoons olive oil

30 g (1 oz) fettucine, broken into 4 cm (1½ in) pieces

100 g (3½ oz) chickpeas (garbanzo beans), soaked overnight in cold water and drained

1.5 litres (3 pints) chicken stock

8 baby carrots, peeled

400 g (14 oz) green peas, shelled (about 1 cup)

1 red capsicum (bell pepper), roasted, peeled and sliced

50 g (1½ oz) oyster mushrooms

salt and cayenne pepper

Fry the fettuccine in hot oil until crisp and golden. Drain on absorbent paper.

Cook chickpeas in a large saucepan with chicken stock over medium heat for 25 minutes or until tender, then add carrots and fresh peas and simmer until vegetables are tender.

Remove from the heat and add capsicum, oyster mushrooms, salt and cayenne to taste. Serve topped with fried fettucine.

Serves 4

couscous and vegetable soup

2 tablespoons olive oil

1 onion, chopped

2 chicken breast fillets, cut into 1 cm (1/2 in) pieces

2 cinnamon sticks

1/2 teaspoon ground cardamom

1/2 teaspoon paprika

1/2 teaspoon chilli powder

1 tablespoon tomato paste

1 x 400 g (14 oz) can tomatoes, drained and chopped

1.5 litres (3 pints) chicken stock

1 zucchini (courgette), chopped

1 carrot, peeled and chopped

4 yellow button squash, quartered

90 g (1/2 cup) couscous

2 tablespoons coarsely chopped coriander (cilantro) leaves

Heat olive oil in a large saucepan, add onion and cook over low heat until soft. Add chicken and cook a further 3 minutes. Add cinnamon, cardamom, paprika and chilli and stir over low heat for 3 minutes until fragrant. Add tomato paste, tomatoes and chicken stock and season to taste. Bring to a simmer, cover and cook over low heat for 10 minutes. Add vegetables and cook a further 15 minutes, or until vegetables are just tender.

Gradually pour in couscous and cook, stirring occasionally, for 5 minutes. Remove cinnamon sticks and serve in warm soup bowls sprinkled with coriander.

Serves 6

pasta and bean soup

This is a wonderful Italian dish *(pasta e fagioli)* made with nutritious borlotti beans. The soup is so wholesome it makes a great one-dish meal served with good crusty Italian bread.

2 tablespoons olive oil

1 carrot, finely chopped

2 sticks celery, finely chopped

1 leek, finely sliced

150 g (5 oz) pancetta, chopped

1 x 400 g (14 oz) can tomatoes, undrained

*200 g (7 oz) dried borlotti beans, soaked in
    cold water overnight*

salt and cracked black pepper

100 g (3½ oz) dried stellette (star-shaped) pasta

1 tablespoon finely chopped sage

1 tablespoon finely chopped flat-leaf (Italian) parsley

3 tablespoons parmesan, shaved

sage leaves fried in olive oil until crisp for garnish

extra olive oil

Combine oil, carrot, celery, leek and pancetta in a large saucepan and cook over medium heat until lightly coloured. Add tomatoes and cook over low heat for 10 minutes. Add the drained beans and 2.5 litres (10 cups) water and bring to the boil. Reduce heat, cover and simmer, stirring occasionally, for 1 hour, or until beans are tender.

Remove ½ cup of beans from the liquid with a slotted spoon and process in a food processor until smooth. Return to the saucepan and stir well. Season to taste with salt and freshly ground black pepper. Just before serving add pasta and simmer for 3–5 minutes, or until pasta is *al dente*. Remove from heat and stir in the herbs.

Ladle into warm soup bowls and garnish with parmesan and crisp sage leaves. Serve with extra olive oil at the table.

Serves 6

scallop and
lemongrass soup

1 litre (2 pints) fish stock

250 ml (1 cup) tomato juice

1 stick lemongrass, white part only, cut in half
   lengthwise and bruised

100 g (3½ oz) dried rice vermicelli

1 tomato, peeled, seeded and chopped

2 teaspoons grated ginger

½ teaspoon palm sugar

1 clove garlic, finely chopped

20 fresh scallops

salt and pepper

8 basil leaves

Heat stock, tomato juice and lemongrass in a large saucepan until boiling. Simmer for 3 minutes, remove lemongrass and add vermicelli. Simmer for 2 minutes.

Add tomato, ginger, sugar, garlic and stir to combine. Simmer for 2 minutes.

Add scallops and simmer for about 2 minutes or until scallops are just cooked. Add salt and pepper to taste. Serve topped with torn basil leaves.

Serves 4

udon noodle soup
with vegetables

Dashi Stock
8 cm (2½ in) piece kombu (dried seaweed)
1.5 litres (3 pints) water
20 g (¾ oz) dried bonito flakes

100 g (3½ oz) daikon (see glossary)
400 g (14 oz) dried udon noodles
1 tablespoon mirin
5 tablespoons soya sauce
6 fresh shiitake mushrooms, sliced
100 g (3½ oz) bamboo shoots, sliced
12 spinach leaves
2 teaspoons grated ginger
4 spring onions (scallions), finely sliced

To make the dashi stock, heat seaweed in water. Remove seaweed just before boiling point. Add bonito flakes and bring back to the boil, then remove the pan from the heat immediately. Leave for 30 seconds and strain through a very fine strainer.

Cut daikon into 1 cm (½ in) slices and boil for 5 minutes. Drain, then cut into quarters.

Place noodles in a large pan of boiling water and simmer for about 10 minutes or until cooked. Remove and drain.

Bring dashi to the boil in a large pan and add mirin and soya sauce. Add mushrooms and simmer until tender. Add daikon, bamboo shoots, spinach leaves and ginger and bring back to the boil. Add noodles to the soup and bring to the boil. Remove from the heat and serve in 4 soup bowls. Garnish with spring onions.

Serves 4

fried pizzettes with caramelised onion, baby prawns and rocket

coriander and chilli cornbread

wonton wrapped tiger prawns

herb, cheese and artichoke pastries

parmesan crisps

tartare of tuna with wasabi dressing on avocado cream

bruschetta with borlotti beans and olives

warm cheese and chilli dip

chicken-filled rice paper rolls

monkey bread

schiacciata with rosemary

strawberries on toast

spicy deep-fried quail

warm oysters with chervil butter sauce

chilli crisps

pissaladière

to have with drinks

fried pizzettes
with caramelised onion, baby prawns and rocket

1½ teaspoons dried yeast

125 ml (½ cup) warm water

185 g (1⅓ cups) plain (all-purpose) flour

1 teaspoon salt

1 tablespoon light olive oil

2–4 tablespoons vegetable oil for frying

20 g (1½ tbs) unsalted butter

3 small red onions, finely sliced

1 small bunch rocket (arugula), shredded

200 g (7 oz) cooked small prawns (shrimps),
   shelled and deveined

Dissolve yeast in warm water.

Combine flour, salt, olive oil and yeast mixture in a food processor until mixture forms a ball. Transfer to a floured surface and knead for 5 minutes, or until dough is smooth and elastic. Place in a lightly oiled bowl, cover with greased plastic wrap and set aside in a warm place for 1½ hours, or until doubled in size. Punch down dough and roll out on a floured surface to 5 mm (¼ in) thickness. Cut out rounds with a 4 cm (1½ in) biscuit cutter.

Heat vegetable oil in a frying pan and cook the dough rounds over medium heat until golden and cooked through. Drain on absorbent paper.

Melt butter in a saucepan and cook onion over low heat for 20–25 minutes, or until caramelised. Top pizzette rounds with onion, rocket and prawns. Serve warm or at room temperature.

Serves 6

coriander and chilli
cornbread

2 large eggs (60 g)
110 g (½ cup) caster (superfine) sugar
225 g (1½ cups) plain (all purpose) flour, sifted
3 teaspoons baking powder
170 g (1 cup) cornmeal (polenta)
2 fresh red chillies, finely chopped
*2 tablespoons freshly chopped coriander
  (cilantro) leaves*
a pinch of salt
250 ml (1 cup) milk
100 g (½ cup) butter, melted

Preheat the oven to 210°C (410°F).

Beat eggs and sugar until pale and fluffy.

In a separate bowl, combine flour, baking powder, cornmeal, chilli, coriander and a pinch of salt. Gently stir in combined milk and butter. Add egg mixture and stir briefly to combine. Pour into a greased and floured 20 cm (8 in) square cake tin and bake for 30 minutes or until cooked when tested with a skewer. Stand in the tin for 5 minutes before turning out onto a wire rack to cool.
Cut into small squares.

Makes about 25

wonton wrapped
tiger prawns

24 green (raw) tiger prawns (shrimps),
  shelled and deveined, tails intact

6 tablespoons soya sauce

2 tablespoons coriander (cilantro) roots, finely chopped

1 clove garlic, finely chopped

24 wonton wrappers

1 egg, beaten

48 strands fresh egg noodles

vegetable oil for deep-frying

Chinese plum sauce or sweet chilli dipping sauce
  (available at supermarkets and Asian food stores)

Marinate prawns in soya sauce with coriander root and garlic for 15 minutes. Drain.

Wrap each prawn in a wonton wrapper, leaving the tail exposed. Seal with egg. Tie 2 fresh egg noodles around each prawn.

Deep-fry in hot vegetable oil until prawns just change colour. Drain and serve hot with plum or chilli sauce.

Makes 24

herb, cheese and artichoke pastries

6 sheets filo pastry

150 g (5 oz) unsalted butter, melted

Filling

120 g (¾ cup) freshly grated parmesan

200 g (7 oz) oil-marinated artichoke hearts, drained and finely chopped

3 tablespoons mayonnaise

2 tablespoons flat-leaf (Italian) parsley, finely chopped

1 tablespoon fresh oregano, finely chopped

2 drained anchovy fillets, finely chopped

1 clove garlic, finely chopped

¼ teaspoon cayenne pepper

Preheat the oven to 180°C (350°F).

To make the filling, combine ingredients, season to taste and mix well.

Cut each sheet of pastry into 8 rectangles about 12 cm x 15 cm (5 in x 6 in). Cover with a damp tea-towel. Brush one rectangle of pastry with butter. Place a teaspoon of filling diagonally across one corner of pastry and roll up, folding in ends to enclose filling as you would for a spring roll. Roll up and seal with a little of the melted butter. Place on a tray and cover with a damp tea-towel. Repeat with remaining pastry and filling. (Pastries can be frozen at this stage; defrost before cooking.)

Place pastries on a lightly greased oven tray, brush tops with a little melted butter and bake for 12–18 minutes until golden and crisp. Serve hot or at room temperature.

Makes 48

| **parmesan** crisps

160 g (1 cup) Parmigiano-Reggiano, finely grated
3–6 rocket (arugula) leaves, finely chopped

Heat a non-stick frying pan over medium heat. Sprinkle a little cheese lightly over the pan in 2–3 circles of about 6 cm (2½ in) in diameter, then sprinkle with a little chopped rocket.

Cook 1–2 minutes, or until cheese melts and begins to bubble. Remove gently with an egglift and immediately drape crisps over the handle of a wooden spoon to shape. Set aside to cool.

Repeat with remaining ingredients.

Makes 20–24

tartare of tuna
with wasabi dressing
on avocado cream

1 tablespoon wasabi powder

2 tablespoons water

*100 ml (scant ½ cup) sashimi shoyu sauce
or light soya sauce*

2 tablespoons chopped chives

3 ripe avocados, halved, stoned and peeled

1½ tablespoons lemon juice

125 ml (½ cup) pouring cream

½ teaspoon sansho (Japanese pepper) or white pepper

salt to taste

*900 g (1¾ lb) sashimi-grade yellowfin tuna, cut into
2 cm (¾ in) pieces*

crackers or biscuits for serving

mustardcress or watercress leaves to garnish

Combine wasabi powder with water and mix to a paste. Add shoyu sauce and chives and stir to combine.

Combine avocado, lemon juice, cream, *sansho* and salt to taste in a food processor and process until smooth. Cover with plastic wrap and refrigerate for 1 hour.

Gently mix tuna with wasabi mixture. Spoon avocado mixture onto crackers or biscuits, top with a piece of tuna and sprinkle with mustardcress or watercress leaves to garnish.

Makes approximately 36

bruschetta with
borlotti beans and olives

200 g (7 oz) dried borlotti beans,
    soaked in cold water overnight

2 sprigs fresh thyme

1 stick celery, thickly sliced

185 ml (¾ cup) olive oil

1 clove garlic, chopped

½ red onion, very finely chopped

1 tablespoon oregano

2 tablespoons lemon juice

salt and pepper

1 small baguette

80 g (½ cup) small black olives, pitted
    and coarsely chopped

Combine drained beans, thyme and celery in a large heavy-based saucepan and cover with water. Bring to the boil and cook over medium heat for 25–30 minutes or until beans are tender. Drain and discard thyme and celery.

Place half the beans in food processor with 60 ml (¼ cup) of the olive oil and the garlic and process until smooth. Transfer to a bowl, stir in remaining beans, onion, oregano and lemon juice and season to taste.

Cut bread into 2 cm (¾ in) thick slices, brush with a further 60 ml (¼ cup) of the oil and grill on both sides until golden. Spread bean mixture on bruschetta, drizzle with remaining oil and top with chopped olives.

Makes 12–14 slices

warm cheese
and chilli dip

40 g (2 tablespoons) butter

1 clove garlic, finely chopped

1 small brown onion, chopped

*4 canned small jalapeño chillies, drained
and finely chopped*

1 teaspoon ground cumin

1 tablespoon plain (all-purpose) flour

250 ml (1 cup) chicken stock

100 g (3½ oz) soft cream cheese, chopped

120 g (¾ cup) parmesan, grated

165 g (5½ oz) cheddar, grated

salt and pepper

1 tomato, seeded and chopped

Melt butter in a saucepan, add garlic and onion and cook over low heat until onion is soft. Add chilli, cumin and flour and stir over heat for 1–2 minutes, then stir in chicken stock and simmer for 5 minutes. Add cheeses, season to taste and stir over low heat until smooth and well combined.

Spoon into a serving bowl, top with chopped tomato and serve with blue corn or plain corn chips.

Serves 6–8

chicken-filled rice
paper rolls

1–2 chicken breast fillets (depending on size)
1 tablespoon olive oil
12 rice paper rounds
1 head butter lettuce
1 capsicum (bell pepper), cut into strips
1 carrot, peeled and cut into strips
75 g (1 cup) beansprouts
24 mint leaves
hoisin sauce

Pan-fry chicken breast fillets in olive oil over medium heat until cooked. Cool and cut into strips. Dip rice paper briefly into hot water and drain. Top rice paper with a small lettuce leaf, capsicum and carrot strips, beansprouts and mint leaves. Fold sides in and roll up firmly. Serve with hoisin sauce for dipping.

Makes 12

monkey bread

This bread is of middle European origin and one of the most delicious starters to serve at a barbeque. It is not sliced; guests just break a piece from the loaf and enjoy it still warm from the oven. The recipe comes from one of Australia's most respected cooking teachers, Marieke Brugman, who owns Howqua Dale Gourmet Retreat in Victoria with co-owner Sarah Stegley.

450 g (3 cups) plain (all-purpose) flour
7 g (1 sachet) dried yeast
35 g (⅓ cup) powdered milk
1 tablespoon olive oil
1 tablespoon sugar
1 teaspoon salt
250 ml (1 cup) lukewarm water

Butter Mixture
100 g (3½ oz) melted butter
45 g (⅓ cup) sesame seeds
¼ teaspoon salt
40 g (¼ cup) poppy seeds
2 cloves garlic, crushed
1 tablespoon finely chopped coriander (cilantro) leaves
1 small fresh red chilli, seeded and finely chopped

For butter mixture, combine all ingredients. Preheat the oven to 180°C (350°F).

Combine the rest of the ingredients in a large bowl and stir in lukewarm water. Bring ingredients together to form a dough and knead on a lightly floured surface for about 10 minutes until smooth and elastic. Place dough in a lightly oiled bowl and turn to coat with oil. Cover with plastic wrap and stand in a warm place until doubled in size.

Turn dough out on a lightly floured surface and knead until smooth. Break off walnut-size pieces of dough and shape into balls. Dip balls in butter mixture and place, closely packed, in a layer on the base of a buttered 21 cm (8 in) rum baba cake tin or savarin tin. Top with another layer, then drizzle with the remaining butter mixture. Cover with plastic wrap and stand in a warm place until increased in size by two-thirds. Bake for about 1 hour until well browned and loaf sounds hollow when tapped. Serve warm.

Serves 6

schiacciata with rosemary

Giuliano Bugialli has been honoured both in Italy and the United States for his outstanding contribution to the art of Italian cooking. I tasted this delightful bread during one of Giuliano's many visits to Australia.

Schiacciata is similar to focaccia and this florentine version can be flavoured with sage or rosemary. It is perfect with a chilled Campari and soda.

1 sachet (7 g) dry yeast
250 ml (1 cup) lukewarm water
335 g (2¼ cups) plain (all-purpose) flour
salt and freshly cracked black pepper
2 heaped tablespoons fresh rosemary leaves
2 tablespoons olive oil

In a small bowl, dissolve yeast in lukewarm water. Place flour in a mound on a large board. Make a well in the flour and pour in dissolved yeast and add a pinch of salt. Using a fork, slowly incorporate all but 3 or 4 tablespoons of the flour. Knead dough for 10–15 minutes until smooth. Sprinkle dough with remaining flour and place in a large bowl. Cover and rest in a warm place until doubled in size (about 1 hour).

Alternatively the yeast mixture and flour can be processed in the food processor with salt until mixture forms a ball. Remove and knead on a lightly floured surface until smooth and elastic, then cover and rest in a warm place.

Preheat the oven to 220°C (425°F).

When the dough has risen spread it onto a large lightly greased oven tray (25 cm x 35 cm/ 10 in x 14 in). Sprinkle with rosemary, salt, plenty of black pepper and olive oil. Rest covered again until it has almost doubled in size (about 45 minutes). Bake for 20–25 minutes or until crisp and cooked. Slice into fingers and serve while hot.

Serves 6

strawberries on toast

A great accompaniment to chilled champagne. Australian native pepperberries are small dark purple aromatic berries with a strong pepper heat. If unavailable substitute freshly cracked black pepper.

250 g (1 punnet) strawberries
250 ml (1 cup) orange juice
1 tablespoon balsamic vinegar
3 tablespoons sugar
1 baguette, cut into 12–14 slices
200 g (7 oz) goat's cheese
1 tablespoon ground native pepperberries or to taste

Poach hulled strawberries in orange juice, balsamic vinegar and sugar for 3–4 minutes or until tender. Remove and drain.

Grill slices of baguette and spread with goat's cheese. Top slices with strawberries and sprinkle with native pepper before serving.

Makes 12–14

spicy deep-fried quail

8 quails

2 tablespoons Chinese five-spice powder

2 fresh small red chillies, seeded and finely chopped or to taste

1 tablespoon salt

80 ml (⅓ cup) olive oil

vegetable oil for deep-frying

Remove leg, thigh and breast portions from quail.

Combine five-spice powder, chilli and salt in a bowl and mix well. Brush quail portions with olive oil, toss in spice mixture, then cover and refrigerate for 30 minutes.

Deep-fry quail, in batches, in hot oil for about 2 minutes or until golden and cooked. Drain on absorbent paper.

Makes 32 pieces

warm oysters with
chervil butter sauce

A skiing holiday in picturesque Sun Valley, California wouldn't be complete without a cooking lesson or two. I first tasted a variation of this wonderful oyster recipe at Tante Marie's School in San Francisco where Jean Pierre Moullè was teaching.

200 g (7 oz) unsalted butter
2 spring onions (scallions), finely chopped
250 ml (1 cup) dry white wine
salt and freshly ground pepper
1 small leek, very finely sliced
1 stick celery, julienned
1 carrot, julienned
rock salt
24 oysters in the shell
2–3 tablespoons fresh chervil, chopped

Place 1 tablespoon of the butter in a saucepan and melt over low heat. Add spring onions and stir until soft. Add wine and boil for 3–4 minutes or until reduced by half. Stir in the strained oyster juices. Whisk in the remaining butter, a small piece at a time, over low heat until the sauce thickens. Add salt and pepper to taste.

Blanch leek, celery and carrot briefly in boiling salted water. Drain and refresh under cold water. Drain again. Spread rock salt on a large platter, arrange oysters in shell on top of salt. Place vegetables on top of oysters and drizzle with butter sauce. Top with finely chopped chervil.

Serves 4

149

| chilli crisps

12 square egg-pastry wonton wrappers
   (available from Asian food stores)
1½ tablespoons salt
3 teaspoons chilli powder, or to taste
vegetable oil for deep-frying

Cut each wonton wrapper into 3 triangles.

Using a mortar and pestle, pound salt and chilli powder to a fine powder. Deep-fry pastry triangles in hot vegetable oil until crisp and golden, then drain on absorbent paper. Sprinkle crisps with chilli mixture and serve hot or at room temperature. Can be kept in an airtight container for 2 days.

Makes 36

pissaladière

The Côtes-du-Rhône region in southern France produces exceptional red wines perfect for enjoying with a slice of pissaladière, the French answer to the Italian pizza. Meg Jump of Entreveux is a warm friendly cooking teacher specialising in provençal dishes, and a week spent in her kitchen learning the secrets of this colourful robust cuisine was delightful. The huge bay windows in the kitchen were thrust open each morning allowing the sun and overhanging vines to spill in onto the kitchen bench. It also provided a magnificent view of the old citadel above the village.

A glass of Côtes-du-Rhône-Villages Red (AOC) from Rasteau was a perfect match with a warm slice of this tasty traditional onion tart which often includes tomatoes when made in the villages close to Italy.

125 g (¾ cup) plain (all-purpose) flour
½ sachet (3.5 g) dried yeast
¼ teaspoon salt
1 tablespoon olive oil
4–5 tablespoons warm water

Topping
6 tablespoons olive oil
1 kg (2 lb) red onions, finely sliced
1 clove garlic, finely chopped
bouquet garni made from 2 bay leaves, 2 sprigs thyme and 2 sprigs parsley
salt and cracked black pepper
120 g (¾ cup) black olives, pitted and halved
8 anchovies

Place flour, yeast, salt and olive oil in the bowl of a food processor and process to combine. With motor running gradually add warm water until mixture forms a ball. Remove and place in an oiled bowl. Cover with a damp tea-towel and leave to rise in a warm place for 30–45 minutes or until doubled in size.

For topping, heat oil in a large pan and fry onions and garlic over low heat with the bouquet garni for about 45 minutes or until very soft and caramelised. Remove herbs and add salt and pepper.

Preheat the oven to 220°C (450°F).

Roll out the dough thinly to a round shape about 32 cm (13 in) in diameter and spread on an oiled pizza tray. Prick all over with a fork. Brush the edges with olive oil and arrange the onion mixture on top leaving a 1 cm (½ in) border around the edges. Garnish with black olives and anchovies and bake for 20–30 minutes or until cooked. Cut into wedges and serve hot.

Makes 8 slices

glossary

Arborio rice
An Italian wide-grain rice with a soft texture and chalky centre. Traditionally used for making risotto.

Balsamic vinegar
A speciality vinegar from Italy that is fermented in oak barrels. It has a distinctive caramel flavour.

Black bean paste
A paste made from salt-fermented and dried soya beans, often with the addition of chilli or garlic.

Bocconcini
A stretched curd cheese with a pliable smooth texture.

Bok choy
Bok choy has many names, including Chinese chard and pak choy. It has thick, crisp white stems with dark green leaves and is similar to silverbeet. Sold in bunches.

Bonito flakes
Shaved dried fish flakes used to make dashi, Japanese stock.

Bouquet garni
A combination of herbs used for flavouring stocks and soups usually comprising a bay leaf, sprig of thyme and parsley.

Chilli jam
Can be purchased in major supermarkets and Asian food stores. Made by cooking chillies, herbs and spices and adding palm sugar, tamarind water and fish sauce, which is simmered until it reaches a jam consistency.

Chinese rice vinegar
Made from fermented rice and is milder and sweeter than white-wine vinegar.

Choy sum
Also known as Chinese flowering white cabbage. Has pale green, tender fleshy stems with rounded pale to mid-green leaves and small yellow flowers at the tips of the inner stems. The stems have a distinctive, slightly bitter flavour and are often preferred to the leaves.

Cloud-ear fungus
Also known as black fungus or wood-ear fungus, this edible fungus is sold dried. It needs to be soaked in water before use. Texture is gelatinous.

Coriander
Also known as cilantro and Chinese parsley. All parts of this herb are used: the seeds are popular in curry powders and spice mixes, the roots are used in Thai curries, and the leaves are added to many Asian dishes.

Couscous
Made from semolina granules and water, and is widely used in Middle Eastern cooking.

Curly endive
A frizzy-leafed vegetable with a slightly bitter taste. Also called escarole and frisée.

Curry paste, Thai green
Basic ingredient in Thai cooking made from a blend of herbs, spices and green chillies.

Curry paste, Thai red
Basic ingredient in Thai cooking made from a blend of herbs, spices and red chillies. Both green and red curry paste can be purchased in major supermarkets and Asian food stores.

Daikon
Japanese name for the large white radish used in Asian cooking.

Dashi
Japanese stock base made from *kombu* (dried seaweed) and flakes of dried bonito.

Fish sauce
Also known as *nam pla* (Thai) and *nuoc mam* (Vietnamese). This salty brown aromatic liquid is made from fermented shrimps and has an unpleasant pungency which disperses on cooking.

Flat-leaf parsley
Also called Italian parsley or continental parsley and has dark green leaves.

Gai-lan
Also known as Chinese kale and Chinese broccoli. It has dark green leaves, thick stems and small white flowers. The vegetable can be steamed, braised or stir-fried.

Galangal
Also called Thai ginger, this spicy aromatic rhizome resembles ginger in appearance and is a pink–yellow colour with an aroma similar to camphor.

Ginkgo nut
The hard-shelled kernel of the fruit of the maidenhair tree.

Hoisin sauce
A thick reddish-brown Chinese sauce which is sweet and spicy. Can be used in stir-fries, grills and braises.

Japanese eggplant
A small slender purple eggplant (aubergine).

Kaffir lime leaves
Highly aromatic leaves from the kaffir lime tree. The leaves are used extensively in South-East Asian cooking. The dark, glossy two-petalled leaves have an intense citrus flavour.

Kecap manis
A thick, sweet Indonesian dark soya sauce.

Kombu
Dried seaweed or kelp.

Lebanese cucumber
A small dark green cucumber with tender skin, pale green flesh and small seeds.

Lemongrass
A very fragrant grass-like plant. Lemongrass adds a citrus flavour to dishes and is available fresh, dried or in brine.

Lotus root
The edible rhizome from the lotus plant. When young it is peeled and eaten fresh in salads. The more mature roots are simmered in soups, stuffed or stir-fried.

Mirin
A clear sweet liquid brewed from fermented rice. Used sushi rice and as a flavouring.

Native pepperberries
These Australian berries are small, dark purple and very aromatic with a strong pepper heat.

Noodles
Bean thread noodles
Transparent noodles made from mung bean flour, also known as glass noodles, cellophane noodles and bean thread vermicelli.

Egg noodles
Available in a variety of thicknesses. Readily available at Asian supermarkets fresh and dried.

Hokkien mee
Round medium thick yellow noodles also known as stir-fry noodles.

Rice noodles
Fresh noodles come in a variety of widths and are also known as *hor fun* or *he fen* in China. Dried noodles or rice sticks come in thin threads, vermicelli, or flat ribbons.

Shanghai noodles
Fresh flat noodles similar to hokkien but paler in colour. Generally sold fresh and unoiled. Available in Asian supermarkets.

Soba noodles
Slender Japanese buckwheat noodles, popular in soups, or served chilled with a dipping sauce.

Somen noodles
Thin white Japanese noodles made from wheat and traditionally eaten cold or served in warm broth.

Udon noodles
Japanese wheat noodles available fresh and dried and may be round, square or flat.

Palm sugar
Made from the sap of the coconut palm which is heated to form crystals. Most commonly sold in rounded cake form.

Pancetta
This is the same cut of pork as bacon but cured in salt and spices, not smoked.

Pea shoots
The growing tips and top set of leaves of a pea plant.

Radicchio
A bitter red-leaf salad vegetable from the chicory family.

Red onion
These onions have a deep reddish purple skin and are also known as Spanish onions. They vary in shape from spherical to oval.

Rocket
Also known as arugula, rughetta, roquette and rucola, this spicy salad leaf is best used when young and tender. The mature leaves become very hot and peppery.

Sambal oelek
Also called *ulek,* this hot sambal is made from salt, vinegar or tamarind and pounded chillies.

Sansho pepper
Japanese pepper.

Shallots
Small onions with red or copper coloured skin. Several small bulbs grow together on a single plant; they have a sweet and mild flavour.

Shoyu sauce
Japanese soya sauce made with soya beans and wheat. It is less salty and lighter in colour than Chinese soya sauce.

Snowpeas
These flat podded small-seeded peas are also known as mange-tout.

Spring onions
Also known as green onions and scallions. They are slender, and the whole plant – from the barely formed white bulb to the green tops – is used in Asian cooking.

Star anise
A dried star-shaped seed pod with a licorice flavour. It is one of the ingredients of Chinese five spice powder.

Tamarind
The tamarind tree produces seed pods which are used extensively in South-East Asian cooking. Can be purchased as a concentrate or pulp and is used as a souring agent and tenderiser for meat.

Tofu
Pressed curds of soya bean milk. Also known as beancurd.

Tomato passata
Crushed or puréed tomatoes.

Verjuice
Partially fermented grape juice.

Wasabi paste
Also known as Japanese horseradish, this pungent pale green root is sold in powder and paste form.

conversions

Solid Weight Conversion

Metric	Imperial
15 g	½ oz
30 g	1 oz
60 g	2 oz
90 g	3 oz
125 g	4 oz (¼ lb)
155 g	5 oz
185 g	6 oz
200 g	7 oz
250 g	8 oz (½ lb)
280 g	9 oz
300 g	10 oz
345 g	11 oz
375 g	12 oz (¾ lb)
400 g	14 oz
450 g	15 oz
500 g	16 oz (1 lb)
750 g	24 oz (1½ lb)
1 kg	32 oz (2 lb)

Liquid Conversions

Metric	Liquid	Cups
30 ml	1 fl oz	
60 ml	2 fl oz	¼ cup
125 ml	4 fl oz	½ cup
150 ml	5 fl oz	
175 ml	6 fl oz	
250 ml	8 fl oz	1 cup

Metric	Liquid	Cups
300 ml	10 fl oz	
375 ml	12 fl oz	
500 ml	16 fl oz	2 cups
600 ml	20 fl oz (1 pint)	2½ cups
1 litre	1¾ pints	
1.25 litres	2 pints	

Standards

½ teaspoon	2.5 ml
1 teaspoon	5 ml
1 tablespoon	20 ml

All spoon and cup measurements are level.

1 American tablespoon = 15 ml

Oven Temperatures (use as a guide only)

Temperatures	Celsius	Fahrenheit	Gas Mark
very slow	120	250	1
slow	150	300	2
moderately slow	160	325	3
moderate	180–190	350–375	4
moderately hot	200–210	400–425	5
hot	220–230	450–475	6
very hot	240–250	500–525	7

Note: All butter used is salted unless stated otherwise.

index

acknowledgments

Many years ago I received a phone call from Charlie Lockhart, then editor of *Vogue Entertaining* magazine, asking if she could write a feature on my visit to Marcella Hazan's cooking school in Bologna. Since that day she has become a wonderful friend and is now the accomplished editor of *Australian Gourmet Traveller* magazine. My grateful thanks go to her for permission to publish the recipes originally printed in *Australian Gourmet Traveller*.

A loving thank you to my dear friends, Nancy Pilcher, previously Editor-in-Chief of *Vogue* magazine, and Robyn Holt, previously editor of *Vogue Living*, for their encouragement and confidence in me as a food writer. Without them this book would not have evolved.

Thank you also to the enthusiastic team at HarperCollins*Publishers*, Helen Littleton, Jacquie Brown and Judi Rowe, for their support.

It has been a pleasure to work with photographer Louise Lister and stylist Karen Cotton, thank you both.

The greatest thanks of all are due to my husband Richard, who has enthusiastically tasted a million noodle and pasta recipes, and my daughter Kate, and son Carter for their candid opinions.

I would also like to thank the following people for their inspiration, friendship and recipes: Chalie Amatyakul; Ron Bendall; Paul Blain; Glen Bowman; Marieke Brugman and Sarah Stegley; Giuliano Bugialli; Biba Caggiano; Bronwen Clark; Sue Dodd; Gabriele Ferron; Annie Foord; San Gajaseni; Celestino Giacomella; Valentina Harris; Marcella Hazan; Alex Herbert, Hyatt Regency Hotel Singapore; Luis Irizar; Meg Jump; Jean Pierre Moulle; Gary O'Callaghan; Angelo Parracucchi; Luciano Parolari and Jean Govoni Salvadore; Richard Purdue; Carol Selva Rajah; Fulvia Sesani; Kathy Snowball; Rosa Russo, Tasting Places; Carla Tomasi; and Joanne Weir.

Thanks also to the following for generously supplying props for photography: Accoutrement, Mosman, NSW; Funkis, Bondi, NSW; Orson and Blake, Woollahra, NSW; The Bay Tree Kitchen Shop, Woollahra, NSW.

recipe credits

Grateful thanks to the following for permission to use their recipes:
Recipe on page 145 originated from Giuliano Bugialli, *The Fine Art of Italian Cooking*, Random House, New York, 1997; recipe on page 16 originated from Biba Caggiano, *Northern Italian Cooking*, HP Books, Italy, 1981; recipe on page 44 originated from Valentina Harris, *Valentina's Italian Regional Cookery*, BBC Books, London, 1990, and recipe on page 11 originated from *What Pasta, Which Sauce*, Kyle Cathie, UK, 1998; recipes on pages 3 and 42 originated from Marcella Hazan, *The Classic Italian Cookbook*, Macmillan, London, 1990, and on page 48 from *More Classic Italian Cooking*, Alfred Knopf, New York, 1978; recipe on page 123 originated from Angelo Parracucchi's *Cucina Creativa All'Italiana*, Sperling and Kupfer Editori, Italy, 1986; recipe on page 13 originated from Jean Govoni Salvadore, *Cooking Ideas from Villa d'Este*, Villa d'Este SpA, Cernobbio, 1981; recipes on pages 22 and 27 originated from Carol Selva Rajah; recipe on page 6 originated from Fulvia Sesani; recipes on pages 14 and 101 originated from Carla Tomasi; and recipes on page 45 and 56 originated from Joanne Weir.

Recipes by Lynne Mullins on pages 4, 9, 10, 30, 33, 36, 63, 66, 72, 76, 86, 92, 107, 110, 112, 113, 120, 121, 123, 126, 132, 133, 134, 136, 137, 139, 140, 141, 142, 147, 148 and 150 were first published in *Australian Gourmet Traveller*.